The End of White World Supremacy

The End of White World Supremacy

Four Speeches by Malcolm X

**Edited and with an
Introduction by
Imam Benjamin Karim**

ARCADE PUBLISHING — New York

Little, Brown and Company
BOSTON   TORONTO   LONDON

ARCADE

Library of Congress Catalog Card Number 89-80486

ISBN: 1-55970-006-8

Published in the United States by Arcade Publishing, Inc., New York,
a Little, Brown company, by arrangement with Seaver Books, New York.

10   9   8   7   6   5   4   3   2   1

Published simultaneously in Canada
by Little, Brown & Company (Canada) Limited

PRINTED IN THE UNITED STATES OF AMERICA

*To Nicholas, Zaid,
Tariq, Khalid, Alex,
and Nathalie, who can,
if they learn to love,
forestall Armageddon.*

Contents

Introduction
by Imam Benjamin Karim

Malcolm X was Minister of Temple Number 7, at Lenox Avenue and 116th Street, from 1952 to December, 1963. Temple Number 7—earlier known as the Muhammad Temple of Islam and later as Muhammad's Mosque Number 7—was the most important Muslim temple in America, outside of the Chicago headquarters, and Malcolm, as its spiritual leader, was Elijah Muhammad's most articulate disciple. In addition to his temple lectures, which in the early days he delivered personally three times a week, Malcolm wrote regular columns for a number of black or black-oriented newspapers, and thus was widely known to at least a certain segment of the black community. But until 1957 he was virtually unknown to the public-at-large, that is to say White America, which pays little or no heed to black activities so long as they don't spill over or threaten the white *status quo*.

I, like most blacks—or "Negroes" as we then called ourselves—had heard of Malcolm X prior to 1957, but my idea of him was confused and, undoubtedly, erroneous. I vaguely knew him to be a black nationalist and the leader of the religious group called the Muslims, who were often referred to in Harlem as "God's Angry Men." What brought them, and Malcolm as their leader, to my attention was an incident that occurred early in the spring of 1957.

Late in the evening of April 26, 1957, three men, two of whom were later identified as Muslims, were witness to an altercation between the police and a man the police had accused of beating an unidentified woman. As the police started working over their victim, a man named Reese Poe, the three men began to remonstrate with them. "You're not in Alabama," one of the Muslims, Hinton Johnson, was reported to have called out, "this is New York." At first the police merely ordered Johnson and his companions to move on. When they refused they were placed under arrest and taken to the 28th Precinct station house, but not before one of the policemen, Patrolman Mike Dolan, had hit Johnson with his nightstick.

The subsequent chain of events, which is worth relating in detail for a number of reasons, was reported as follows by *The Amsterdam News:*

> A woman who had witnessed the incident then rushed to the Moslem restaurant on Lenox Avenue and told the Moslems that one of the brothers had been beaten by a policeman.
>
> A group of Moslems, led by their spiritual leader Minister Malcolm X, then went to the station house and asked to see their brother. Mr. X claims that the police first told him that they did not have such a man in the station.
>
> But as the word passed through Harlem the Moslem crowd swelled around the station house and finally police admitted that they did have the Moslems inside.
>
> The Moslems asked to see their brother. Mr. X was per-

mitted to see Hinton. He claims that Hinton told him that when he had been brought into the station house he was suffering from the blows of the nightstick and that in his pain he fell down on his knees to pray.

He told Mr. X that when he was on his knees praying in the station house the lieutenant in charge came upon him and hit him across the mouth with a nightstick and also hit him on his shins with the stick.

Mr. X demanded that Hinton be sent to a hospital for attention. Police finally agreed and sent him to Harlem Hospital.

While he was being treated there the Moslems, joined by a group of Nationalists and other Harlemites, congregated into a crowd of 2,000 outside the hospital.

As the crowd grew, police rose to the emergency and all available cops were pressed into duty, with Deputy Inspector McGowan taking command.

Then, to the surprise of all, Hinton was released from Harlem Hospital and taken back to the 28th Precinct, where he was placed in a cell.

The Moslems followed. They formed a solid line half a block long in front of the 123rd Street station house and waited orders from their leaders. Their discipline amazed police, and more than one high-ranking officer expressed growing concern.

By this time Mr. X was in the station house with his attorney, Charles J. Beavers of 209 W. 125th Street. They arranged for bail for Pots and Tall * and then asked to see Hinton.

When Attorney Beavers saw Hinton's condition he immediately asked that he be sent to the hospital, charging that he was in no condition to remain in jail.

But police flatly refused, saying that he had already been to the hospital. They said Hinton must remain in a cell for arraignment in court Saturday morning. . . .

---

* The other two men arrested with Hinton Johnson.

It was 2:30 A.M. by this time. But the Moslem followers were still in front of the station house. Mr. X left the station house, gave one brief command to his followers, and they disappeared as if in thin air.

One amazed policeman, on seeing this, said: "No one man should have that much power!"

What the policeman—who was later identified by the writer of the article, James Hicks, as being Deputy Inspector McGowan himself—meant, of course, was: "No one *black* man should have that much power." But it was that same power and presence which so impressed and frightened the police that also attracted me and thousands of other young so-called Negroes to Malcolm. Here was a man who could walk boldly into the jaws of the lion, walk proud and tall into the territory of the enemy, the station house of the 28th Precinct, and force the enemy to capitulate. Here was a man who could help restore the heritage, the pride of race and pride of self, that had been carefully stripped from us over the four hundred years of our enslavement here in White America. I knew, when I first heard of the Hinton Johnson incident, that, at the very least, I had to go and hear this man. But before relating, briefly, my first contact with Malcolm, it is worthwhile detailing the subsequent events of that weekend, for what they reveal about Malcolm's stubborn devotion to his followers and about the methods of the police in Harlem.

After the crowd had dispersed, a number of Muslims assembled, at 4:00 A.M., at the restaurant they own on Lenox Avenue to discuss the matter. Malcolm, it was reported, made the decision that they would not appear en masse at Hinton Johnson's arraignment the following day. Malcolm appeared, however, together with the attorney Charles Beavers and another Muslim, Mr. John. The editor

of *The Amsterdam News*, James Hicks, was also present.
As Hicks relates:

Here again the police irritated the Moslems by attempting
to arraign Hinton without his lawyer being present. Actually
they did put him on bail while Attorney Beavers was in
Judge Baers court on another case.

After bail was set at $2,500, without Hinton's lawyer being
present, the Moslems quickly put up the bail money and
stood outside where they were told Hinton would be delivered to them.

But instead of Hinton being delivered to them he was
turned loose in the building to find his way out alone.

He came out of the jail staggering, bleeding, and alone.
This enraged the Moslems.

They then rushed him to Dr. Leona Turner in Long Island. She took one look at him and ordered him to the hospital at once. Back sped the car across the island to Manhattan, and Hinton was finally admitted to Sydenham.

There it was found that he had a clot on the brain, that
he was bleeding internally. Hospital authorities gave him a
50–50 chance to live.*

As he battled for his life, the Moslems gathered again
Sunday. This time in daylight in the square opposite Sydenham Hospital. They marched around the square protesting,
and police soon discovered they had been joined by Moslems
from Boston, Hartford, Baltimore, Washington, and Wil-
mington.

Though they were stern in their protest, they were as or-
derly as a battalion of Marines.

With the crowd growing around the hospital, the Moslems
were joined by some teen-agers carrying zip guns. As soon
as this was learned, Mr. X once more dismissed his followers

---

* Hinton Johnson survived—with the help of a metal plate in-
serted in his skull. A court subsequently awarded him $70,000, the
largest award ever made in a case of police brutality.

and sent them home. He stated that it was not their intention to start any violence.

But Monday, as Hinton's life hung in the balance, reports spread through Harlem that if Hinton died there would be a riot in Harlem Monday night.

Police prepared for the worst. High police officials arranged a meeting with Mr. X at an uptown location.

In the meeting he openly stated that his followers were ready to die when mistreated. But he insisted that they were not "looking for trouble."

"We do not look for trouble," he told police officials. "In fact we are taught to steer clear of trouble. We do not carry knives or guns. But we are also taught that when one finds something that is worthwhile getting into trouble about, he should be ready to die, then and there, for that particular thing."

. . . At the meeting it was brought out that the Moslems have a witness, Harry Buffins, who is prepared to testify that an officer wearing shield number 2775 said in front of Harlem Hospital Friday night: "I'd have shot the nigger but the other cops kept getting in my way."

The witness will also testify that an officer pointed at Mr. X and said: "We should break that bastard's head because he is their leader."

One of the things that added to the tension Friday night was that all officers involved in the Lenox Avenue fracas were white. . . .

It was this incident that really brought Malcolm X and the Muslims to my attention. I read about it in the papers and heard about it on the radio. Malcolm X! That "X" really struck me, and I kept repeating it to myself, as though there was something magic about it. And I kept thinking about what Malcolm had said about not looking for trouble but, when you find something really worthwhile getting into trouble about, being willing to die then and there for it. They were strong words, fighting words, and yet what impressed me most about Malcolm's handling of the Hinton Johnson affair was his firmness with the white police—they knew he meant what he said—and the way he not only failed to stir up trouble but actually prevented it.

At that time, in April of 1957, I was working downtown for a recording company. I had my hair conked (and it had turned red from the sun) and wore a little goatee, trying very hard to be hip. A brother by the name of Leo used to come around all the time trying to interest me in the Muslims and trying to get me to read black history. In those days, I was caught up in astronomy and visiting museums. But black history? I didn't even know there was one worth worrying about, much less reading about.

Nonetheless, after the Hinton Johnson episode some of the things that Leo had talked to me about, which earlier had fallen on deaf ears, began to pique my curiosity. I couldn't remember whether he had talked to me specifically about Malcolm, but he had tried very hard to get me to come to the mosque. Now I decided to go.

I went one day—it was a Sunday—with a friend of mine from my home town. What struck me most about our arrival was the fact that we were searched. No one likes being frisked, and I was no exception. They didn't actually search my pockets, but they ran their hands down my clothes to see if I had any concealed weapons on my person. And they stood very close to see whether I had any alcohol on my breath. If I had been carrying any weapons they would have taken them away from me, not so much perhaps because they were afraid of nonbelievers—what Malcolm called "lost-founds"—causing trouble but because it had always been a custom among the Muslims not to allow any dangerous weapons into the mosque. If I had

had alcohol on my breath, I would have been turned away, for they did not want anyone in the mosque who was drunk, or even who had been drinking.

Inside, what struck me immediately was the "uprightness," the sobriety of the brothers walking around. I am not sure whether the first impression was favorable or unfavorable, but I am sure that with my conked hair in contrast to their close-cut haircuts and my dress and demeanor quite different from their sober, dignified air, I was not fully at ease.

When Malcolm came to the rostrum his first words were, "As-Salaam-Alaikum"—"Peace be unto you"—which I had never heard before and which struck me as strange. Black people have—or had at the time—an aversion to foreign names, foreign words and languages. Whenever we would hear Africans talking—or Japanese or Chinese—we would laugh and make fun of them. We thought they were talking gibberish. Why couldn't they speak a civilized tongue like English? What we had failed to realize, of course, and Malcolm helped to make clear for us, was that this was part of the conditioning process to keep us unaware of our own heritage and language.

After his greeting, Malcolm began teaching. His subject that night was slavery, the slave history of America, and I was spellbound. Now I understood for the first time why brother Leo had been after me to learn black history. I had never in my life heard a man speak like that, and I knew then that something in my life had changed, or was about to change. I had been like a boat adrift, and I had found my course. Malcolm must have talked for well over two hours, but it passed so quickly it seemed like a matter of minutes. When he had finished, he asked if anyone had any questions. I may have had some, but my head was spinning, and besides I was too shy to stand up and ask any. Then Malcolm said:

"How many of you would like to join onto your own kind? It will cost you nothing. All you have to do is be black and brave. I know you're black. Let's see how brave you are!"

I got up and followed the brothers toward the rear. There the secretary of the mosque explained to us what we had to do, in a very simple manner. There was no ritual. All you had to do was affirm that you believed what you had heard, that you believed it was the truth. In addition, you had to copy a letter, before officially receiving your "X," stating that you had attended meetings and believed in the truths you had heard. Although you only had to copy the letter, it had to be copied exactly. I wrote the letter nine times before I finally got it correct. That may seem a minor annoyance, being made to copy a letter so many times, but it was part of a discipline, part of learning to concentrate.

Six months after I began coming to the mosque I received my "X"—which of course is substituted for the slave name given to our forebears by the plantation owners, "X" being the unknown factor, since we did not know what our rightful names were. Since there had been another Benjamin to receive an "X" before me, my new name became Benjamin 2X. By the time this happened I was a changed person, inside and out. I got my hair cut and began to look like those other brothers I had noted with a mixture of curiosity and concern that first day at the mosque. I was never much of a drinker, but now I drank not at all. I had been a fairly flamboyant dresser, but now I dressed soberly. I had been a great curser, but now I stopped completely. I had been a pork eater, and now I

stopped completely. I had once read somewhere that profanity is an attempt of a lazy, feeble mind trying to express
itself forcibly, but until I became a Muslim the words
seemed to make no impact upon me. It was as though I
had been reborn, a new person. Through Malcolm I had
seen a great light, and for the next seven years I was to
be the devoted disciple of the Muslims, and of Malcolm.

There were three lectures a week at Mosque No. 7—two
in the evening during the week and one on Sunday at 2:00
P.M. Even before I had officially received my "X" I spent
so much time at the mosque that people thought I was
already a member. In those days Malcolm would speak at
all three sessions, and there was always standing room
only. Often as many as a thousand people came, and many
were the times when people had to be turned away. After
the Hinton Johnson incident, however, Malcolm became
a national figure and began to do a lot of traveling. Thus
he needed assistant ministers not only for Temple No. 7,
but also to visit and lecture at the various places where,
partly thanks to the national coverage he had received, new
mosques had been founded.

Malcolm set up classes to prepare others to help and fill
in for him. It was a kind of Muslim university, which emphasized public speaking but also taught history, geography, current events (both national and international), and
Bible concordances. Malcolm set the class up, and in the
early days presided over it. Later he chose me to take it
over, when the pressure of traveling became too great for
him to continue on any kind of regular basis. He chose me,
I suppose, because I was, if not the best, at least the hard-
est working student. Later I traveled a great deal myself,
substituting for Malcolm at various mosques when he himself could not be present. And, often, I would "open up"

for him when he was the main speaker at Mosque No. 7. "Opening up" meant, really, a speech in itself, ranging in time from half to three-quarters of an hour, preparing the audience for Malcolm's message. It was, in a sense, warming the audience up, so that when Malcolm began they would already be attuned to the essence of what he wanted to say.

I remember very clearly the day that Malcolm X delivered the speech entitled "Black Man's History," which comprises the first section of the present volume. It was a speech also referred to as "Yacub's History." I opened up for him that day, and this may be as good a time as any to describe an opening. The first thing I did was welcome the audience to the mosque and lead them in prayer. I would ask the audience to stand and stretch forth their hands, as the Muslims pray. The only thing we did not do was go through the prostrations.

For the newcomers in the audience, the most perplexing aspect of the mosque was the blackboard on the rostrum itself. On the left side of the blackboard was drawn an American flag, and beneath it were written the words: SLAVERY, SUFFERING & DEATH. To the right was a painting of a black man hanging from a tree, and on the far right was a Muslim flag with star and crescent and, in each of the four corners, the letters I F J E, which stood for Islam, Freedom, Justice, and Equality. Written out beneath the flag were the last three of these words while, in the center of the board, was written: WHICH ONE WILL SURVIVE THE WAR OF ARMAGEDDON? What I did that day, as I generally did, was explain what the words and symbols on that blackboard meant. The SLAVERY, SUFFERING & DEATH referred to what we had received here in America. We have suffered and been put to death—physically, spiritually, and mentally. Islam was the force that would free us from the chains of physical and spiritual slavery. A man, I would explain, cannot be free if his mind is not free. Once his mind is free, he will free himself.

Then I would talk a bit about the question: WHICH ONE WILL SURVIVE THE WAR OF ARMAGEDDON? Black people who are Christians are taught, and believe, that the war referred to is war between spiritual forces, between the concepts of good and evil. We taught that the war is one that will take place on this earth, a war between the oppressed and their oppressors—a race war. It will be a race war simply because the oppressor is by and large white, except for the nonwhites he has pressed into his service. It will be a war in which there will be a winner, a war where one side will survive and the other perish. In this war, this final war, in the final phases of this final war, no prisoners will be taken: all of which relates, and brings us back, to the prophesy in the Bible which we know as the War of Armageddon.

Having explained the words and symbols on the blackboard, I would then generally move on to one of Malcolm's favorite notions. He always stressed etymology, going back to the roots and sources of things, and one of the words he dissected was the word "Negro," trying to explain why we had been taught to call ourselves Negroes. Most of us knew it came from the Spanish, that it was an adjective meaning "black," but Malcolm taught that it was allied to and derived from the prefix "necro-" meaning "death," "corpse," "dead tissue." So I would write the word "nekropolis," which is the Greek form for "necropolis," explaining that we were a dead people living here in the wilderness of North America, and that what had put us to death was our sojourn here in slavery. Then I would go to the Bible and take this prophesy of Abraham that the Jews apply to themselves, where it says (Genesis 15:13): "Know of a surety that thy seed shall be a stranger in a land that is not theirs, and shall serve them; and they shall afflict them four hundred years. And also that nation, whom they shall serve, will I judge. And afterward shall they come out with great substance."

Then, depending on the time allotted me and the subject of Malcolm's lecture, I would go into history—Egyptian history, world history, archaeology—trying to impress on the audience, as Malcolm had taught, the importance of history to us, that history of which we had been systematically deprived.

I remember clearly that day in December 1962. While I was opening up I saw Malcolm come in, carrying his tan briefcase that bore in gold letters the name, Malik El Shabazz. He first spoke with some officials, then walked over to the secretary's compartment, opened his briefcase, took out some cards or a small notebook and began making some notes. Something about the way I was opening up seemed to catch his attention; he stopped what he was doing and walked over to beneath the clock directly opposite me about fifty feet across the auditorium. He put his left hand under his right elbow and cocked his right arm, holding his notebook to his ear to hear what I was saying. I was fully aware of his presence and, as always —how I don't know—I knew that he approved of what I was saying. He never needed to let me know in so many words; I could always tell instinctively whether he approved or disapproved.

I also noted as I talked that day that he was wearing his blue suit and red tie. This was his "burning suit," which he wore when he was fully prepared and intended to give a very deep lecture. After a few minutes he walked back over to the secretary's compartment and said something to Captain Joseph. Then they both began walking toward the rostrum, with Captain Joseph on Malcolm's right. This was a habit with Malcolm when approaching the rostrum: he was concentrating on what he was going to say, and generally asked the captain or one of his lieutenants to accompany him to the speaker's platform.

Malcolm climbed the couple of steps to the rostrum and sat down behind me at a little table. I went on developing whatever point I was making, knowing that no matter what I might be expounding on I would be expected to interrupt whenever Malcolm indicated he was ready. When I heard the words behind me, "Make it plain," that was my cue to cut it short, and I would finish up as gracefully and quickly as possible, then introduce Malcolm. He disliked any kind of long-winded or flowery introduction, so I said, merely: "Now I bring before you Brother Minister Malcolm X, who will give you a better knowledge and clearer understanding of The Honorable Elijah Muhammad, what he is teaching here in the wilderness of North America."

Six months after his lecture at Temple No. 7, Malcolm was invited, in June of 1963, by Adam Clayton Powell to speak at the Abyssinian Baptist Church. At that time, Powell had opened up his church to what he called a Black Forum, inviting all shades and opinions of black thought to come and speak their minds freely. He invited the nationalists, the heads of the African Nationalist movement, he invited other ministers and heads of various Negro organizations, and, of course, he invited Malcolm. I say "of course," but the fact is that Powell was one of the few ministers with the courage to ask Malcolm to lecture at his church. Most Negro preachers are very careful about whom they invite to speak to their congregations. But Powell is more independent, more courageous than most and, besides, I suspect he liked Malcolm. I think he saw a little of himself in Malcolm. The feeling was mutual, I might add, for Malcolm respected Powell, and admired his intelligence and independence. However they may have differed on some matters, they saw eye-to-eye on many of the basic problems facing all black people in America: better housing, better schools for their children, equal job opportunities, etc. Where they differed, no doubt, was on the long-term solutions. At the time he made this speech at the Abyssinian Baptist Church, Malcolm was very strongly for separation of the races. There has never been a time in the history of the world when the slave masters have ever made their slaves their equals, and Malcolm was convinced that America in the 1960s was no exception. Some people would dispute this, saying: "Look at all the progress we have made since 1865." To which Malcolm would inevitably reply: "The only progress we have made is as consumers. We still don't manufacture anything, we still don't legislate for ourselves. Our politics is still controlled by white people, our economy is still controlled by white people, therefore we have no real say about our future." Malcolm, perhaps more than any other black leader, was as much concerned about the future as about the immediate problems confronting his people. He tried to make his audiences think not only of the present generation but also of their children's children, and their children after them. There were people who said that Malcolm was not being realistic when he talked about separation, but they failed to realize that in stressing this con-

cept he was preparing for the future, thinking of the unborn generations yet to come.

This second speech, "The Black Revolution," is an
interesting contrast to the "Black Man's History," in
many ways. In the earlier speech, which lasted for about
two hours, the entire audience of over a thousand people
was so quiet throughout that you could have heard a pin
drop. In the speech at the Abyssinian Baptist Church,
which was less than half as long, the audience responded
vocally almost from the beginning to Malcolm's words,
in an emotional give and take. Malcolm's mastery of the
Bible is also apparent in "The Black Revolution." He knew
the Bible as well as, and probably better than, most Christian preachers. Here, speaking to a basically Christian
audience—there were perhaps a dozen or so Muslim
brothers present, who had come with Malcolm—Malcolm
begins by clarifying his position: he is a Muslim, speaking
from a religious rather than a political platform. Malcolm,
or the Muslims, referred to the Bible as a "poison book" in
that, for him, it had been used by theologians to poison
the minds of Negroes throughout the centuries. Since
virtually all black people in this country are Christians,
whether they go to church or not, most of Malcolm's audiences, outside of his mosque lectures, were Christians.
Whenever he spoke to Christian audiences, he went on
the assumption that the people he was addressing were
as dead, and that his job was to raise them from the dead,
to cast some light into their darkened minds. Because
he knew the Bible so well, and because he knew exactly
what the black ministers had taught black people out of
the Bible, he would use the Bible to his own good advantage. If black people have only one book to their name,
chances are that book will be the Bible, and most of them

have at least a nodding acquaintance with portions of it. Much of the time Malcolm would use familiar portions of the Bible to illustrate his point, such as his comparing Moses and the slaves in ancient Egypt to our situation here in present-day America. But he also resorted to little known and little understood portions of the Bible. There is one book of the Bible that most black (and I suspect white) preachers shy away from, because it is very confusing and difficult to explain, and that is the Book of Revelation. Malcolm saw in that book, and went to considerable pains to explain it, a parallel and a prophecy, for it deals with the judgment and the destruction of a world, which Malcolm explained in terms of race, of the coming judgment and end of white world supremacy.

If a great number of Malcolm's speeches were made to adult, Christian audiences—predominately or exclusively black—he was also much sought after as a speaker on college campuses. It was said that during the first three years of the sixties, the only speaker more in demand in America on college campuses was John F. Kennedy. "The Old Negro and the New Negro" was the theme of one of his favorite speeches. The version which appears in this volume was delivered in Philadelphia in the fall of 1963. Actually, Malcolm gave essentially the same speech twice on the same day, the first time at the University of Pennsylvania, and again that same evening over a Philadelphia radio station. I was with him at the radio station that evening, and by the time he was halfway through his speech his voice was fading. He had probably talked for six or eight hours that day, and, as often happened with Malcolm, his voice would be hoarse by mid evening. But he had a remarkable gift of recovery, and within a few hours the voice would be back as strong and clear as ever.

At the University of Pennsylvania, of course, Malcolm was speaking to an audience of both blacks and whites. But his manner and the content of his talks were essentially the same whether he was addressing an all black or an integrated student audience. Malcolm believed, by the way, in Student Power: not only did he feel that the college-educated black, if he could retain (as he must) his sense of reality and history, and refrain from being absorbed into the white world by its material enticements, was obviously better equipped to cope with the problems besetting his people in America, but he also believed, or hoped, that the white college student was more receptive to change than were his parents. He believed, and tried to emphasize to white students, that they could not follow in the path of their elders and survive in today's world. To illustrate his point, he reminded them of former Prime Minister Macmillan's press conference in New York in which he spoke of the changing geography of the world, of the decline of empires, saying that in his own lifetime he had seen England, and other Western powers, shrink from vast empires to second-rate powers.

For me, "The Old Negro and the New Negro" paints a beautiful picture of the new thinking prevailing among black people. Malcolm felt that the people were evolving much faster than most of their so-called leaders, and that the leaders would have to catch up with the people. It is this "New Negro" who is causing the moderate leaders to speak more militantly, whether they want to or not. Malcolm once said that the moderate Negro leader is going to wind up more militant than the militants, if only to save his own life. He predicted that black people would become so fed up with their condition, with the hypocrisy and procrastination of the white man, that one would have to be like a lion to lead them, or fall by the wayside. Malcolm predicted that Martin Luther King would change his ways and his tune, and he was right. He also predicted that the young blacks would no longer allow themselves to be exploited and brutalized without fighting back. And he was also optimistic about new black leaders rising up to take his place and the place of others. I have often heard it said what a vacuum Malcolm left, that there is no other leader of his stature on the horizon, and in a sense this is true. But even in death he remains a source of great inspiration, and, as he predicted, I am sure new black leaders will arrive, drawing on him as a source of strength, seeing in him a symbol of what one man can do.

One final point: what struck me most about Malcolm's visits to campuses was the open-minded attitude of his listeners wherever he went. There were some exceptions, of course. I remember once when Malcolm was speaking at Harvard, a man got to his feet during the question-and-answer period and, although Malcolm had said nothing anti-Semitic in his speech, equated him to Hitler. "You're a racist," the white student screamed, going on to list all the crimes that Hitler had committed against the Jews. Malcolm answered him by saying that racism had been going on in this country long before Hitler had been born, that he was not a racist but someone simply telling the truth about what was happening here in this country. And if America has problems today, he said, they are race problems, and until these are solved America will continue to be beset by internal strife.

But most students, black and white, received his message openly, and after a lecture would crowd around him, asking him all kinds of questions. I always had the feeling that the students were not only impressed by him but that they really liked him, and this was true of every college he visited.

"God's Judgment of White America" was the last speech Malcolm gave while still a member of the Nation of Islam, on December 4, 1963. Mr. Muhammad had been scheduled to speak, but he had had to cancel and Malcolm suggested that he speak in his place, in order not to disappoint the crowd. Unlike most of his speeches, which though prepared and thought out in Malcolm's mind were delivered extemporaneously, this speech was typed. In it Malcolm dwells at some length on the March on Washington, using it to illustrate what he considered the failure of Negro leadership, showing how cooperative ventures with whites invariably turn into co-opted ventures. This march started out as an all-black march, then it became an integrated march, and soon the whites were in complete charge. Malcolm points out that the whole affair was controlled. People had to arrive at a certain time, march at certain times between two presidents—Washington and Lincoln—and leave at a certain time. He notes that some black leaders whose speeches were known to be antagonistic to the Kennedy administration were not allowed to speak.

One important point that should be made about the Manhattan Center speech: this is the speech that has come to be known as "The Chickens Are Coming Home to Roost" speech, because of Malcolm's use of this term in the course of the evening. But readers of the speech may be surprised not to find it anywhere in the body of the text. That is because Malcolm used the phrase in response to a question from the audience.

A week or so earlier, just after President Kennedy's assassination, Mr. Muhammad had given strict orders that no minister should make any derogatory remark about the dead President. It should be remembered that a great number of black people really loved President Kennedy and, thought the Messenger, to attack him might create enemies not only for the Muslims but for black people in general. When a minister speaks, he is not speaking personally but for all Muslims and for the Messenger: he is expressing the attitude and thought of the Nation of Islam.

Following the speech, Malcolm was called to Chicago by Mr. Muhammad, after which his suspension was announced. It was a ninety-day suspension, to run through March 4, 1964. I have heard it said that the Messenger used Malcolm's derogatory reference as an excuse for suspending him, that there were basic differences between them and this was an easy way of solving them. Personally, I have never believed these stories. I believe Mr. Muhammad took the disciplinary action he felt he had to, as a father disciplines a child he loves, knowing that if he comes through the trial he'll be a better man for it, but also knowing there is a chance he'll lose him if he doesn't come through. One thing that most people forget is that the Nation of Islam continued to exist after Malcolm was gone, that as powerful and magnetic a force as Malcolm was—and he was personally responsible for bringing a great many people into the Nation of Islam—the fact remains that the people were not for the most part following Malcolm, they were following The Honorable Elijah Muhammad. I'm not pretending that Mr. Muhammad taught Malcolm everything he knew, but he did give him the keys to knowledge and understanding. This is one key point in Malcolm's life that is still generally misunderstood, or overlooked.

These four speeches are only a fragment of Malcolm's thought, of course, but taken together they do represent a fair cross section of his teaching during that crucial last year as a leader in the Nation of Islam. They are the words of an impassioned and inspired man who, in spite of the portraits painted of him by the mass media during his lifetime, did not spend his adult life looking for trouble, but who, when he found something worthwhile getting into trouble about, stood ready to die for it, then and there.

January, 1971

Black Man's History

I want to thank Allah for coming and giving to us our leader and teacher here in America, The Honorable Elijah Muhammad. I want to thank Brother Benjamin at the outset for doing a wonderful job of opening up our eyes and giving us a good preliminary basic understanding of the means and the objectives of The Honorable Elijah Muhammad, and also I am thankful to Allah for bringing so many people out here tonight, especially just before Christmas. You know, it's next to a miracle when you get this many of our people together so close to Christmas interested in anything whatsoever that's serious. And actually what this shows is the change that's taking place among the so-called Negroes not only here in New York but throughout the entire world. Today dark mankind is waking up and is undertaking a new type of thinking, and it is this new type of thinking that is creating new approaches and new reactions that make it almost impossible to figure out what the black man is going to do next, and by black man we mean, as we are taught by The Honorable Elijah Muhammad, we include all those who are nonwhite. He teaches us that black is the basic color, that black is the foundation or the basis of all colors. And all of our people who have not yet become white are still black, or at least part of the Black Nation, and here at Muhammad's Mosque when you hear us using the term "black" we mean everbody who's here, regardless of your complexion. If you're here at the Mosque you're black, because the only ticket you need to get into Muhammad's Mosque is to be black. So if you got in you know you're black. You may not have known that you were black before you came here. In fact, very few of our people really look upon themselves as being black. They think of themselves as practically everything else on the color spectrum except black. And no matter how dark one of our people may be, you rarely hear him call himself black. But now that The Honorable Elijah Muhammad has been teaching among the so-called Negroes, you find our people of all complexions going around bragging that "I'm a black man." This shows you that a new teaching is taking place and there is new thinking among the so-called Negroes. Yet just yesterday you would have to admit that it was very difficult to get our people to refer to themselves as black. Now all of a sudden our people of all complexions are not apologizing for being black but bragging about being black. So there's a new thinking all over America among the so-called Negroes. And the one who is actually the author of this new thinking is The Honorable Elijah Muhammad. It is what he is teaching that is making our people, for the first time, proud to be black, and what's most important of all, for the first time it makes our people want to know more about black, want to know why black is good, or what there is about black that is good.

I might stop right here to point out that some of you may say, "I came up here to listen to some religion, about Islam, but now all I hear you talk about is black." We don't separate our color from our religion. The white man doesn't. The white man never has separated Christianity from white, nor has he separated the white man from Christianity. When you hear the white man bragging, "I'm a Christian," he's bragging about being a white man. Then you have the Negro. When he is bragging about being a Christian, he's bragging that he's a white man, or he wants to be white, and usually those Negroes who brag like that, I think you have to agree, in their songs and the things they sing in church, they show that they have a greater desire to be white than anything else. My mother was a Christian and my father was a Christian and I used to hear them when I was a little child sing the song "Wash Me White as Snow." My father was a black man and my mother was a black woman, but yet the songs that they sang in their church were designed to fill their hearts with the desire to be white. So many people, especially our people, get resentful when they hear me say something like this. But rather than get resentful all they have to do is think back on many of the songs and much of the teachings and the doctrines that they were taught while they were going to church and they'll have to agree that it was all designed to make us look down on black and up at white.

So the religion that we have, the religion of Islam, the religion that makes us Muslims, the religion that The Honorable Elijah Muhammad is teaching us here in America today, is designed to undo in our minds what the white man has done to us. It's designed to undo the type of brainwashing that we have had to undergo for four hundred years at the hands of the white man in order to bring us down to the level that we're at today. So when you hear us often refer to black in almost a boastful way, actually we're not boasting, we're speaking of it in a factual sense. All we're doing is telling the truth about our people. Whenever you exalt black, that's not propaganda; when you exalt white, *that's* propaganda. Yet no one can give biological evidence to show that black actually is the stronger or superior of the two if you want to make that kind of comparison. So never think ill of the person whom you hear representing The Honorable Elijah Muhammad if an overemphasis seems to be placed on the word black, but rather sit and analyze and try to get an understanding.

The Honorable Elijah Muhammad teaches us that of all the things that the black man, or any man for that matter, can study, history is the best qualified to reward all research. You have to have a knowledge of history no matter what you are going to do; anything that you undertake you have to have a knowledge of history in order to be successful in it. The thing that has made the so-called Negro in America fail, more than any other thing, is your, my, lack of knowledge concerning history. We know less about history than anything else. There are black people in America who have mastered the mathematical sciences, have become professors and experts in physics, are able to toss sputniks out there in the atmosphere, out in space. They are masters in that field. We have black men who have mastered the field of medicine, we have black men who have mastered other fields, but very seldom do we have black men in America who have mastered the knowledge of the history of the black man himself. We have among our people those who are experts in every field, but seldom can you find one among us who is an expert on the history of the black man. And because of his lack of knowledge concerning the history of the black man, no matter how much he excels in the other sciences, he's always confined, he's always relegated to the same low rung of the ladder that the dumbest of our people are relegated to. And *all* of this stems from his lack of knowledge concerning history. What made Dr. George Washington Carver a *Negro* scientist instead of a scientist? What made Paul Robeson a *Negro* actor instead of an actor? What made, or makes, Ralph Bunche a *Negro* statesman instead of a statesman? The only difference between Bunche and Carver and these others I just mentioned is they don't know the history of the black man. Bunche is an expert, an international politician, but he doesn't know himself, he doesn't know the history of the black people. He can be sent all over the world by America to solve problems for America, or to solve problems for other nations, but he can't solve problems for his own people in this country. Why? What is it that ties our people up in this way? The Honorable Elijah Muhammad says that it boils down to just one word—history.

When you study the history of Bunche, his history is different from the history of the black man who just came here from Africa. And if you notice, when Bunche was in Atlanta, Georgia, during the summer NAACP Convention, he was Jim Crowed, he was segregated, he was not allowed to go in a hotel down there. Yet there are Africans who come here, black as night, who can go into those cracker hotels. Well, what is the difference between Bunche and one of them? The difference is Bunche doesn't know his history, and they, the Africans, do know their history. They may come here out of the jungles, but they know their history. They may come here wearing sheets with their heads all wrapped up, but they know their history. You and I can come out of Harvard but we don't know our history. There's a basic difference in why we are treated as we are: one knows his history and one doesn't know his history! The American so-called Negro is a soldier who doesn't know his history; he's a servant who doesn't know his history; he's a graduate of Columbia, or Yale, or Harvard, or Tuskeegee, who doesn't know his history. He's confined, he's limited, he's held under the control and the jurisdiction of the white man who knows more about the history of the Negro than the Negro knows about himself. But when you and I wake up, as we're taught by The Honorable Elijah Muhammad, and learn our history, learn the history of our kind, and the history of the white kind, then the white man will be at a disadvantage and we'll be at an advantage.

The only thing that puts you and me at a disadvantage is our lack of knowledge concerning history. So one of the reasons, one of the missions, one of the objectives of The Honorable Elijah Muhammad here in America is not only to teach you and me the right religions but to teach you and me history. In fact, do you know that if you and I know history we know the right religion? The only way that you can become confused, that you can become mixed up and not know which religion belongs to God, is if you don't know history. In fact, you have to know history to know something about God. You have to know history to know something about God's religion. You have to know history to know something about God's people. You have to know history to know something about God's plans and God's purposes, and, as I say, the only people who don't know history are the American so-called Negroes. If you know history, for example, you know when you look at this religion right here [writes "Christianity" on the blackboard] the only way you can explain it is to have a knowledge of history.

Why is it called Christianity? It is called Christianity, they say, because it was named after a man called Christ who was born two thousand years ago. Now you know, brothers and sisters, God is an old God, and the world is an old world. The universe has been here a long time. I think all of you would agree that the universe has been here longer than two thousand years. Then you'll also agree that the universe was made by God Himself, that God created the universe. God created the people who are on this earth, God wouldn't create a universe, God wouldn't set a thing up in the sky that makes nine planets rotate around it, all of them inhabited, you and I inhabiting the planet earth upon which we live—God wouldn't have done all this and not given people a religion. God put His religion here at the creation of the universe. In fact, God's religion is older than the universe. Now then, since you agree to this and you'll agree also that Christ was born two thousand years ago, this couldn't have been God's religion. Your knowledge of history tells you that God couldn't call His religion Christianity because Christianity is only two thousand years old. So if this is the case, then what was God's religion called *before* the birth of Christ? Can you see the importance of history? Why, if you didn't know history you'd think that Christianity was God's religion, and you'd be running around here wondering why everybody doesn't practice it. Because some people have a better knowledge of history than others do, it is only the people whose knowledge of history is limited who jump up and say that Christianity is the name of God's religion. If Christianity hasn't *always* been the name of God's religion it isn't *now* the name of God's religion. God doesn't change the name of His religion; God doesn't change His religion; God doesn't change His mind; God's mind is made up from the beginning. He doesn't have to change His mind because He knows all there is to know all the way down the wheel of time. He never has to change His mind, His mind is made up, His knowledge is complete, all encompassing. Do you understand? So once you can see, and I think you can, then it's almost impossible for God to call *Christianity* His religion.

What should God call His religion? Christians are the ones who call God's religion Christianity, but God was here before Christians came on the scene. They tell you that Christians began back there with the Romans, with one of the Roman Emperors who accepted the teachings of some of Jesus' disciples and then named what the disciples taught "Christianity." But Jesus didn't call it Christianity, it wasn't named until two or three hundred years after Jesus was dead. Right or wrong? Any history book will tell this, any theologian knows this, and the only Negroes who will contend this are those who don't know history, and most Negroes don't know history. Most Negroes will contend this, but when you tell it to the white man he shuts his mouth because he knows that this is true.

Then those who have studied a little deeper will say, "Before God called it Christianity it was called Judaism" —isn't this what they say? Named after a man called Judah. This doesn't follow logically. If Christianity was named after Christ was born, and before Christ was born the religion was called Judaism, then that means that it got its name from a son of Jacob whose name was Judah. But history tells us that Jacob was bending down before Judah was born, which shows us that Jacob's religion couldn't have been Judaism, and Isaac was Jacob's father and he was bending down also before Jacob, his son, was born. Isaac was Judah's grandfather and Abraham was Judah's great-grandfather, meaning that Abraham was on the scene long before Judah, and you couldn't call

Abraham's religion Judaism because there was no such thing as Judaism in Abraham's day. There was no such thing as Judaism in Isaac's day, or in Jacob's day. Do you understand? So what was God's religion before they called it Judaism? This is something that the white man has never taught you and me. The white man is afraid to let you and me know what's God's religion was called in Abraham's day because Abraham is supposed to have been the father of all of them. He is supposed to have been the progenitor of all of them. He is supposed to have been one of God's first servants. One of the first to submit to God is supposed to have been Abraham. Now if you can see this, then find out what Abraham's religion was.

The Honorable Elijah Muhammad teaches us that Abraham's religion was the religion of Islam. Islam only means complete submission to God, complete obedience to God. Abraham obeyed God. Abraham obeyed God so much so that when God told Abraham to take his son and sacrifice him—stick a dagger in his heart, isn't that what he said?—Abraham took his only son up on the mountain. He was going to sacrifice him to God, showing that he believed in Islam. What does Islam mean? Obey God. Submit to God. So that this name [writes "Islam"], if you'll notice, has no connection, no association, with the death of a man. This is not a man's name, this doesn't come from a man. Buddhism is named after a man called Buddha; Confucianism is named after a man called Confucius—right or wrong? Likewise with Judaism and Christianity. But Islam is not connected with any name. Islam is independent of any name. Islam is an act which means submit completely to God, or obey God. And when you say your religion is Islam that means you're a Muslim. So to clarify this what must you do? You must have a knowledge of history. If you don't have a knowledge of history you'll run around calling yourself a Christian when you're serving God, or you'll run around saying your religion is Judaism and you'll swear you're serving God. If your religion is Christianity you're following Christ, if your religion is Judaism you're following Judah, if your religion is Buddhism you're following Buddha, do you understand? And they are all dead, and if you follow them you'll die too. This is where it all leads you. Wherever your leaders go, that's what happens to you. Now we who follow The Honorable Elijah Muhammad, we believe in Islam, we don't believe in Muhammad.

He teaches us the religion of Islam. Do you understand the difference? These people who follow Christ [pointing to the cross painted on the blackboard], they believe in Christ; they believe Christ is God—Oh yes, they do—that he was born of the Blessed Virgin, didn't have a father, was just a spirit, and then came into the world and was crucified, rose from the dead, and went up into space. They believe that, but they believe it because they don't know history. But if you notice, the Jews have a better knowledge of history than the Christians do, do they not? The Christians' history only goes back two thousand years; the history of the Jews goes back beyond four thousand years. Can you see this? And the Muslim history goes back . . . there is no limit to the Muslim history. If you notice, the Christians can only go back to what they call the Greek Empire. That's what they call the Occidental, the beginning of the Occident, the Greek Empire, the Roman Empire, and so forth. The Jews have a knowledge of history that goes back into Egypt and Babylon. You notice how one goes back further than the other. But now the Muslims' history goes back . . . it has no limit. There are no chains on how far you can go back when you are a Muslim. The Christians and the Jews combined go back to whom? To Adam, and they stop right there. And they say beyond him there was nothing happening. The greater their knowledge of history is—this has an influence on the type of religion that they accept. Do you understand?

All praise is due to Allah. Another example: What makes the royal family of Europe, or any country, differ from the peasant? Royalty knows its ancestry, royalty knows its history, this is what makes them royal. You can't have a king who can't trace his history back to his forefathers. The only way you can be king is to be born a king. If you take away his history, and he doesn't know who his forefathers were, what does he become? A peasant—a common ordinary man. Same with the Jews and Christians. It's because the Jews have the longest record of history that they can call themselves the Chosen People. The Christians can't call themselves the Chosen People because their history is not long enough. They can't go back to the time when the choice was being made. The Hebrews, the so-called Jews, can go back so far they can lay claim to that which is actually not theirs. But the reason they can claim it is that nobody else they are dealing with can go back far enough to disprove them. Except the Muslims —do you understand? So The Honorable Elijah Muhammad's mission is to teach the so-called Negroes a knowledge of history, the history of ourselves, our own kind, showing us how we fit into prophecy, Biblical prophecy. When you go to one of the churches you will notice that it is named after some word in their Bible: Big Rock Baptist Church, or Drinking at the Well Baptist Church, Friendship Baptist Church, Union Baptist, Israel Baptist, Jacob's Ladder Baptist. They find some kind of old funny word in their Bible to name their whole religion after. Their whole doctrine is based on a verse in the Bible: "He rose."

The Honorable Elijah Muhammad bases what he teaches not on a verse but on the entire book. And from beginning to end, he says, he can open up the Book and prove that the Bible agrees with him, and then use the Bible to prove that what they are teaching in the church is wrong. You know that's saying something.

For instance, he says that in Genesis, the fifteenth chapter and the thirteenth verse, just to give you an example: "And he said unto Abram, Know of a surety that thy seed shall be a stranger in a land that is not theirs, and shall serve them; and they shall afflict them four hundred years; and also that nation, whom they shall serve, will I judge: and afterward shall they come out with great substance." Now The Honorable Elijah Muhammad says that explains his teachings right there, because he teaches that the so-called Negro is the one that the Bible is talking about. Who have spent four hundred years and are strangers in a land that is not theirs? And you can't deny that we are strangers here. I don't think any of you will deny that we are strangers here. We are not in a country where we are made to feel at home. We'll put it that way. There is hardly any Negro in his right mind who can say he feels at home in America. He has to admit that he is made to feel like a stranger. Right or wrong? Well, this is what God said to Abraham would happen in this day and time. Remember, Abraham's religion was Islam. Abraham wasn't a Jew, Abraham wasn't a Christian, Abraham wasn't a Buddhist, Abraham was a Muslim, which means he obeyed God. God told him, yes, He said, your people are going into bondage, they're going to become slaves, they're going to be afflicted, they'll be strangers in a land far from home for four hundred years. The Honorable Elijah Muhammad says you and I are the seed of Abraham, we're the descendants of Abraham. Now the preacher in the church, he tells you that the Jews are the seed of Abraham. One of them is right and one of them is wrong; either Mr. Muhammad is right and the preacher is wrong, or the preacher is right and Mr. Muhammad is wrong. This is what we are putting on the line today.

Who is the seed of Abraham? Is it this blue-eyed, blond-haired, pale-skinned Jew? Or is it the so-called Negro—you? Who is it? And what makes it so pitiful, many of our people would rather believe that the Jews are God's Chosen People than to believe that they are God's Chosen People. They would rather believe that God is going to save the Jews than believe that God is going to save them. They would rather believe that the Jew is better than anybody else. This is a Negro. Nobody else would put everybody else above him but the Negro. No one likes to place himself below everybody else but the Negro. I mean the American Negro. Remember, God said that the people would be strangers. The Jews aren't strangers. The Jews know their history, the Jews know their culture, the Jews know their language; they know everything there is to know about themselves. They know how to rob you, they know how to be your landlord, they know how to be your grocer, they know how to be your lawyer, they know how to join the NAACP and become the president—right or wrong? They know how to control everything you've got. You can't say they're lost. But the poor so-called Negro, he hasn't control over anything. He doesn't control the NAACP, he can't control the Urban League, he can't control CORE, he can't control his church, he can't control his own schools, he can't control his own businesses in his own community. He can't even control his own mind. He's lost and lost control of himself and gone astray.

But he fits the picture here that the Bible says concerning our people in the last day: "Know of a surety that thy seed shall be a stranger in a land that is not theirs, and shall serve them." And you have served the white man; he hasn't served you and me. Why, the Jew hasn't served anybody here. You are the one that's serving: "And they shall afflict them four hundred years; and also that nation, whom they shall serve, will I judge: and afterward shall they come out with great substance." Ofttimes when you say this to the so-called Negroes they'll come up and tell you that this is the Jew. But if you'll notice, when Jesus was talking to the Jews, way back here in John, he told them that they shall know the truth and it will make them free. The Jews popped up and said: "How are you going to say that we shall be made free? We have never been in bondage to anyone." Isn't that what the Jews told Jesus? Now look at it. If the Jews said to Jesus, two thousand years after Moses supposedly led the Hebrews out of bondage, that they had never been in bondage—now you know the Jews had Moses' history, they knew who Moses was—how could they stand up and tell Jesus they had never been in bondage? Not *these* things that you *call* Jews. They weren't in Egypt, *they* weren't the people that Moses led out of Egypt, and the Jews know this. But the Bible is written in such a tricky way, when you read it you think that Moses led the Jews out of bondage. But if you get a Jew in a good solid conversation today and you know how to talk to him, he'll have to admit this, that it wasn't out of Egypt's land that Moses brought them, that it wasn't out of bondage that Moses brought them— it was out of somewhere else—and where Moses really brought them is their secret, but, thanks to Almighty God, The Honorable Elijah Muhammad knows their secret, and he told it to us and we're going to tell it to you.

If the Bible said that God is going to judge that nation,
the nation that enslaved His people, how would He keep
from destroying His own people? The same Bible is a
book of history and in the eighteenth chapter of the book
of Deuteronomy, in the eighteenth verse, God told Moses:
"I will raise them up a Prophet"—talking about you and
me—I'll raise them up a prophet just like thee—a prophet
like Moses whose mission it would be to do for you and
me the same thing that Moses did back then. It would be
a prophet like Moses. In fact, when you get down to
Malachi, He lets it be known that just before He comes
to judge that nation, the name of the prophet or messenger
whom He would send among the people would be Elijah.
It says: Before the coming of that great and dreadful day
I shall send you Elijah and Elijah's job will be to turn the
hearts of the children to the fathers and the hearts of the
fathers to the children. What does this mean, turn the
hearts of the children to the fathers? The so-called Negro
are childlike people—you're like children. No matter how
old you get, or how bold you get, or how wise you get,
or how rich you get, or how educated you get, the white
man still calls you what? Boy! Why, you are a child in
his eyesight! And you *are* a child. Anytime you have to let
another man set up a factory for you and you can't set up
a factory for yourself, you're a child; anytime another man
has to open up businesses for you and you don't know how
to open up businesses for yourself and your people, you're
a child; anytime another man sets up schools and you
don't know how to set up your own schools, you're a child.
Because a child is someone who sits around and waits for
his father to do for him what he should be doing for himself, or what he's too young to do for himself, or what he
is too dumb to do for himself. So the white man, knowing

that here in America all the Negro has done—I hate to say it, but it's the truth—all you and I have done is build churches and let the white man build factories.

You and I build churches and let the white man build schools. You and I build churches and let the white man build up everything for himself. Then after you build the church you have to go and beg the white man for a job, and beg the white man for some education. Am I right or wrong? Do you see what I mean? It's too bad but it's true. And it's history. So it shows that these childlike people—people who would be children, following after the white man—it says in the last day that God will raise up Elijah, and Elijah's job will be to turn the hearts of these children back toward their fathers. Elijah will come and change our minds; he'll teach us something that will turn us completely around. When Elijah finds us we'll be easy to lead in the wrong direction but hard to lead in the right direction. But when Elijah gets through teaching the Lost Sheep, or the Lost People of God, he'll turn them around, he'll change their minds, he'll put a board in their back, he'll make them throw their shoulders back and stand upright like men for the first time. It says he'll turn the hearts of these children toward their fathers and the hearts of the fathers toward the children. This is something that The Honorable Elijah Muhammad is doing here in America today. You and I haven't thought in terms of our forefathers. We haven't thought of our fathers. Our fathers, brother, are back home. Our fathers are in the East. We're running around here begging the Great White Father. You never hear of black people in this country talking or speaking or thinking in terms of connecting themselves with their own kind back home. They are trying to make contact with the white man, trying to make a connection with the white man, trying to connect, trying to make a connection with a kidnapper who brought them here, trying to make a connection with, actually, the man who enslaved them. You know that's a shame—it's pitiful—but it's true.

The Honorable Elijah Muhammad says that when Elijah comes, the Book says when Elijah comes, what Elijah will do is to teach these people the truth. And the truth that Elijah will teach the people would be so strong it will make all that other stuff that the preachers are talking about sound like a fairy story. Elijah will open the people's eyes up so wide that from then on a preacher won't be able to talk to them—and this is really true. Do you know, people have come to Muhammad's Mosque and no matter whether they believed in what Mr. Muhammad was saying or not they never could go back and sit in church. This is true. What The Honorable Elijah Muhammad does is to turn on the light, and when he turns on the light it enables us to see and think for ourselves. He shows us that what the white man has taught us concerning history has actually been a distortion. He's never given you and me true facts about history, neither about himself nor about our people. You know I read a book one day called *The Four Cities of Troy*. You can go to the library, some libraries, and check it out. What was this based on? To show you what a *liar* the white man is. When I say liar: you have white people who are scientists and keep truth in their own circles, and they never let you—they never let the masses—know anything about this truth that they keep in the circle. They got something else that they invent and put out for the masses to believe, but they themselves keep knowledge in a circle. So in this particular book it pointed out that some archaeologists were delving in the ruins of the ancient city of Troy, and it's the practice of archaeologists to dig, so in digging down into the ruins of Troy they dug deeper than they intended to, and they ran into the ruins of another city that had been there so much longer than this city of Troy that it had gone down beneath the sands of time, and they had built this city of Troy on top of it. When these archaeologists were delving into the ruins of the ancient city they learned that there were ruins of a city more ancient than that. So they started frantically digging into that one and dug some more until they found another one and before they got through digging they had dug down and they had discovered that civilizations in that area had been there so far back into history that at different times in history some of the cities had been destroyed, had become completely covered up with sand and dirt, until another people came along and didn't even know it was there and built another civilization on top of it. This happened four different times—to give you some idea of what the white man knows concerning the length of time man has been on this earth—and still that white man would jump up in your face and try to make you believe that the first man was made six thousand years ago named Adam. And a lot of Negroes will want to know what you are talking about— Adam—that's what God called him—God took some dirt and breathed on it and told Adam, "Come forth," and there he was. Now you know that's a shame. It's all right to believe when you were a little baby that God made a little doll out of the sand and mud and breathed on it and that was the first man. But here it is 1962 with all this information floating around in everybody's ears—you can get it free. Why, you should open up your minds and your heads and your hearts and realize that you have been led by a lie. Today it's time to listen to nothing but naked, undiluted truth. And when you know the truth, as Jesus said: "The truth will make you free." Abraham Lincoln won't make you free. Truth will make you free. When you know the truth, you're free. Also you have your archaeologists, anthropologists, other forms of historians who agree that they don't know how long man has been on earth, but they do know that man has been on earth longer than six thousand years. They know that man was not made just six thousand years ago. They know this now but a long time ago they didn't know it. There was a time when they believed that a man had fewer ribs than a woman. You can believe that because they said that God made Eve from one of Adam's ribs—so Adam had a rib missing. And they actually ran around here believing for many years that man had one less rib, and they were shook up when they got into the science of anatomy and discovered that man—all his ribs were there! They began to wonder then what happened in the Bible?

How long has man been here? In the Bible in the first chapter of Genesis and the twenty-sixth verse, after God had made everything else it says: "And God said, Let us make man." Let me write what God said here on the board . . . Look what God said, brothers. I don't think you ever *looked* at this. It says: "And God said, Let us make man." The key word here is what? Yes, what does "us" mean? More than one. Who was God talking to? If God was all by Himself, no one was there but Him, who was He talking to when He said, "Let us make man"? Who was there with God who was about to help Him make this man? When God was getting ready to make the sun He didn't say, "*Let us* make some sun!" He said, "Let there be light." And here is the sun, a ball of fire 2,679,785 miles in circumference, 853,000 miles in diameter, 14,072 degrees hot, and God said, "Let there be," and that big ball of fire popped up there in the universe, with no help. Now you know something is wrong. It should be harder to make that than a man: a huge ball of fire 2,679,785 miles in circumference, 14,072 degrees hot—that's a whole lot of heat. And God said, "Let there be," and that just jumped up in the universe. He didn't ask for no help: "Let there be this and let there be that." He had so much power that everything He wanted came into existence; as soon as He said "be," there it was. But when He got to man something happened, someone else was there, wasn't there? That's something to think about. We'll let you think about it for a minute . . .

The white man's world is a newer world than the black man's world. If this man said that they were about to make man, and he said we would make him how—in our image—this shows you that there's somebody there with him—in *our* likeness—there is somebody there with him. "Let us make man in our image, in our likeness. Let us make him look like us. He won't be the same as we are, he'll be in our image." That's God talking, right? He's talking to somebody. You know, I'm thankful to Allah for raising up The Honorable Elijah Muhammad and making us see these things that we could never see before. The birth of the white race has always been a secret. The Honorable Elijah Muhammad says that the birth of the white race is shrouded in the story of Adam. The story of Adam hides the birth of the white race, and because you and I have never been taught to look into a thing and analyze a thing we took the story of Adam exactly as it was. We thought that God made *a* man named Adam six thousand years ago. But today The Honorable Elijah Muhammad teaches us that that man, Adam, was a white man; that before Adam was made the black man was already here. The white man will even tell you that, because *he* refers to Adam as the first one. He refers to the Adamites as those who came from that first one. He refers to the pre-Adamites as those who were here before Adam. Right or wrong? Those people who were here before Adam. And he always refers to these people as "aborigines," which means what? BLACK FOLK!!!! You never find a white aborigine. Aborigines are called natives, and they're always dark-skinned people. You and I are aborigines. But you don't like to be called an aborigine; you want to be called an American. Aborigine actually means, "from the beginning." It's two Latin words, "ab" meaning "from"; "origine" meaning "the beginning"; and aborigine is only the term applied to those dark-skinned people who have been on this earth since the beginning of the universe. You know that's going way back. What do you mean, since the beginning of the universe?

The Honorable Elijah Muhammad teaches us that, just as we pointed out a moment ago, the black man has been here a long time. He never has had a beginning. But the white man has never had a knowledge of the history of the black man. It's like a father and a son. If the father is fifty years old and the son is only ten, the father knows everything there is to know about his son because he was here before his son was born; the son only knows what has happened during his own ten years. He only knows what went on before his arrival from what his father tells him. It's the same way with the black man and the white man: the black man's been here a long time, but the white man has been here a short time. Now the white man only knows about himself, what he's been told, and he hasn't been told anything. He came to himself up in the caves of Europe, and he can't get any information that goes beyond the cave. And since you and I fell into his trap and were made deaf, dumb, and blind by him, we don't have access now to any information that the white man doesn't know about. So we think that the beginning of the white man meant the beginning of everything, us too. We're not aware that we were here before he was made. Can you understand that? The Honorable Elijah Muhammad teaches us that sixty-six trillion years ago—trillion, how much is trillion? Not hundreds, nor thousands, nor millions, nor billions, but sixty-six trillion years ago—the black man was here. We have the sun which is the center of the universe; 36,000,000 miles from the sun is the planet we call Mercury, and 67,200,000 miles from the sun is the planet called Venus, and 93,000,000 miles from the sun is the planet here that you and I live on called Earth, 141,500,000 miles out here is a planet called Mars, and 483,000,000 miles from the sun is a planet called Jupiter, 886,000,000 miles from the sun is a planet called Saturn, and on down the road a piece are a couple more planets. So right here this planet that you and I live on called Earth, that rotates around the sun, The Honorable Elijah Muhammad teaches us that sixty-six trillion years ago our people were living on this planet: the black man was living on this planet. But in those days it was larger than it is now, and the planet Mars, that was off here beyond it, had an effect upon our planet then in the same manner that the moon affects us today. At that time there was no moon up there. Where was the moon? The moon was down here, the moon was part of this planet, the moon and this planet were one planet, and the black man was living here then. He was a scientist, he was a wise black man. Black men have always been wise, black men have always been the wisest beings in the universe, and among these beings, black beings, there is one who is supreme; he is referred to as the Supreme Being, do you understand?

So The Honorable Elijah Muhammad tells us that a wise black scientist, sixty-six trillion years ago, began to argue with the other scientists because he wanted the people of Earth to speak a certain language, and since they wouldn't agree he wanted to destroy civilization. So this scientist drove a shaft into the center of the Earth and filled it with high explosives and set it off. He was trying to destroy civilization; he was trying to destroy the black man. But you can't destroy the black man; the black man can't destroy himself. The black man has the most power-ful brain in the universe. So there is no intelligence more powerful than the intelligence of the black man. And be-cause of this the black man can't even create a *thought* that would destroy him. He is indestructible. You can blow up everything and the black man will still be here. You just can't get away from him, brother. So The Honorable Elijah Muhammad said he filled the Earth, the planet, with high explosives and set it off, and when it was exploded the piece that you and I today call the moon was tossed out here into space and it rotated around the Earth. It still rotates around the Earth; it came from the Earth; it was blasted right off the Earth. And as it was blasted right off the Earth, it turned over and over and over and all of the water that was on it stayed with the Earth. So that the piece that was blasted out there has no water on it today, and because it has no water on it it has no civilization on it, has no life on it. You can't have life where there's no water; water is the source of life. Where there's no water there's no life; where there's no life there's no civilization. Can you understand that? So this dead piece, called the moon by us today, turning over and over and over, lost all of its water, all of the water coming with *this* piece. The Honorable Elijah Muhammad told us that this piece, that the Earth, that we remained on, shifted, dropped thirty-six thousand miles in the pocket that we remained in. And as it dropped and all of the water came with it, that left a situation in which today the Earth that we now live on weighs six sextillion tons. The weight of it is six sextillion tons. And as it makes its way around the sun, the strong power of the sun's rays striking the equator causes the planet to turn on its own axis at the speed of 1037⅓ miles per hour. And he teaches us that the square mileage of the Earth is 196,940,000 square miles which means only 57,-255,000 square miles of land stuck up out of 139,685,000 square miles of water. Three-fourths of the Earth's surface is covered with water. Part of the water that left the moon is here with the Earth. So you say since it's the natural law for water to seek its own level, why doesn't it overrun the land? The Honorable Elijah Muhammad says that as the Earth speeds around the sun turning on its axis 1037⅓ miles per hour it creates gravity and the strong attracting power of the sun pulls on the waters of the Earth, drawing them up into the Earth's atmosphere in a fine mist that the naked eye can hardly detect. As this water gathers into the Earth's atmosphere it then distills and comes back to Earth. When it gets heavier than the atmosphere in which it is, it distills and comes back to the Earth in the form of water, rain, hail, or snow. All of the water that you see coming out of the sky went up into the sky. Everything that's coming down on the Earth got up there by leaving the Earth. Do you understand? And he teaches us that it comes back down in the form of hail or rain or snow or whatever else you have, depending upon the temperature of the current atmosphere that it was in. He says that at night the gravitational pull of the moon takes over, and, because the power of the moon is not as great as that of the sun, once the attracting power of the sun is absent at night the moon takes over, but since it can't pull the waters up like the sun does, it still has that magnetic pull and it causes the waves that you see out there on the ocean to churn. It is the moon that does that; the moon makes the waves go up and down. It never lets them level out. If they leveled out the water would overrun the land. It also causes the shifting of the tide. This is the pull of the moon upon the waters of the Earth. If it weren't for the attracting powers of the sun and the moon upon the Earth, the waters would overrun the land and drown out civilization. All of this was done by man himself, not some Mystery God. A black man set this up. And you and I have been running around in the trap that the white man put us in, thinking that the only one who can do anything is a Mystery God and what the Mystery God doesn't do the white man does.

The Honorable Elijah Muhammad says that all the time that this was going on there was no white man. The white man was nowhere on the scene. He says that when the moon was blasted away and we came along with the Earth, one tribe was in fact destroyed. Prior to the time that the explosion took place there were thirteen tribes. In the explosion set off sixty-six trillion years ago the thirteenth tribe was destroyed, and then all of the time down through the wheel of time since then there were twelve tribes until six thousand years ago. And six thousand years ago, a scientist named Yacub created another tribe on this Earth.

Understand, prior to the time the explosion took place, there were thirteen tribes, but the thirteenth tribe was destroyed in that explosion and then six thousand years ago another tribe came on the scene. It was made different from all of the twelve tribes that were here when it arrived. A new tribe, a weak tribe, a wicked tribe, a devilish tribe, a diabolical tribe, a tribe that is devilish by nature. So that before they got on the scene, The Honorable Elijah Muhammad says that when we came with the Earth, the oldest city on the Earth is the Holy City, Mecca, in Arabia.

Mecca is the oldest city on Earth. Mecca is the city that is forbidden. No one can go there but the black man. No one can go there but the Muslims. No one can go there but the believer. No one can go there but the righteous. And at Mecca are kept the records of history that go on back to the beginning of time. He says that fifty thousand years ago another scientist named Shabazz became angry with the scientists of his day. He wanted to bring about a tougher people. He wanted the people to undergo a form of life that would make them tough and hard, and the other scientists wouldn't agree with him. So this scientist named Shabazz took his family and wandered down into the jungles of Africa. Prior to that time no one lived in the jungles. Our people were soft; they were black but they were soft and delicate, fine. They had straight hair. Right here on this Earth you find some of them look like that today. They are black as night, but their hair is like silk, and originally *all* our people had that kind of hair. But this scientist took his family down into the jungles of Africa, and living in the open, living a jungle life, eating all kinds of food had an effect on the appearance of our people. Actually living in the rough climate, our hair became stiff, like it is now. We undertook new features that we have now. The Honorable Elijah Muhammad says that the only hair that the black man has today that looks now like it looked prior to fifty thousand years ago is your and my eyebrows. Right here, you notice, all Negroes have straight—I don't care how nappy their hair is—they have straight eyebrows. When you see a nappy-hair-eyebrowed Negro [chuckle] you got somebody. But all of this took place back in history, and everything The Honorable Elijah Muhammad teaches is based on history. Now then, where does the white man come in?

The Honorable Elijah Muhammad says that the wise

black man who was a master of science never wrote his history like it is written today, of the past. The wise black man in that day wrote his history in the future. The Honorable Elijah Muhammad says that the circumference of the Earth is 24,896 miles, approximately 25,000 miles. So when he says the wise black man of the East writes history a year for every mile, he writes history to last for 25,000 years—not in the past, but in the future. He says that on this Earth there are wise black men who can tune in and tell what's going to happen in the future just as clear— they can see ahead just as clear—as they can see in the past. And every 25,000 years he says that civilization reaches its peak, or reaches its perfection. At this time the wise black man can hear a pin drop anywhere on the planet Earth. And they sit down and write history to last for 25,000 years. After this history expires they put it in a vault at the Holy City, Mecca, and write a new history. This has been going on and on and on. So, in the year one of the cycle in which we now live, he says that in the East there are twenty-four wise men. They're spoken of in the Bible as twenty-four elders or twenty-four prophets or twenty-four scientists or twenty-four imams. Twelve of them are major and twelve of them are minor. So The Honorable Elijah Muhammad says that these twenty-three men are called together by this one, which makes twenty-four. And these twenty-four, these twenty-three presided over by the twenty-fourth, are spoken of in the Book of Revelation where John said he had a vision in heaven where there was a throne, and around the throne were twenty-four seats and on the seats sat twenty-four elders. These twenty-four elders are called angels. They are actually twenty-four wise black men who live right here on this Earth, but no one knows who they are. At the end of every 25,000 years this one calls all of them into conference, and they sit down at the Holy City, Mecca, and he informs them that the history of the past 25,000 years has expired and it's time to write a new history. So these twenty-four, these scientists, begin to tune in on the population of the planet Earth and he says that back in his day—at that time there were five billion people on this Earth—all of them black, not a white man in sight—five billion people—not a white man in sight, so he says that when these twenty-four scientists begin to tune in, they look down through the wheel of time. They can tell not only what the people on this Earth are thinking, but they can tell what their children are thinking, what the unborn children's children are thinking, what the unborn children's children's children are thinking. They can look right down through the wheel of time and tell minute-by-minute, hour-by-hour, day-by-day, week-by-week, month-by-month, year-by-year, for 25,000 years exactly what is going to take place. And they discovered that in the year 8400 to come it would register that among five billion black people, seventy percent would be satisfied and thirty percent would be dissatisfied. And out of that thirty percent would be born a wise black scientist named Yacub, and Yacub would teach among these thirty percent dissatisfied from whom he would come, and create a new race, start a new world, and a new civilization that would rule this Earth for six thousand years to come. So they brought these findings back to the king and they were put in a book. And by the way, that which is written to last for 25,000 years is called the Holy Koran.

The Honorable Elijah Muhammad said that this was put into the history and then when the year 8400 came, Yacub was born. When Yucab reached the age of six years he was playing in the sand one day with two pieces of metal, two pieces of steel, at which time he discovered what is known as the law of magnetism: that unlike attracts and like repels. Two objects that are alike repel each other like two women repel each other, but man and woman attract each other. Unlike attracts and like repels. Yacub discovered this. So Yacub knew that all he had to do was make a man unlike any other man on this Earth and because he would be different he would attract all other people. Then he could teach this man a science called tricknology, which is a science of tricks and lies, and this weak man would be able to use that science to trick and rob and rule the world. So Yacub turned to his uncle and said, "When I grow up I'm going to make a man who will rule you." And Yacub's uncle said, "What can you make other than that which will cause bloodshed and wickedness in the land?" And Yacub pointed to his head and said, "I know that which you know not." Yacub was born with a determined idea to make this man because it had been predicted 8400 years prior to his birth that he would be born to do this work. So he was born with this idea in him, and when his uncle realized that this was he about whom it had been prophesied his uncle submitted. The Honorable Elijah Muhammad said that Yacub went to school in the East; he studied the astronomical sciences, mathematical sciences, and the germination of man. He discovered that in the black man there are two germs. In the black man there's a brown man. In the black man, or the black germ, which is a strong germ, there's a weak germ, a brown germ. Yacub was the first one to discover this and Yacub knew that by separating that brown one from the black one, and then by grafting the brown one from the black one so that it became lighter and lighter, it would eventually reach its lightest stage which is known as white. And when it got to that stage it would be weak, and because it was weak it would be susceptible to wickedness. And then Yacub could take that weak man that he made and teach him how to lie and rob and cheat and thereby become the ruler of all of the rest of the world.

So The Honorable Elijah Muhammad teaches us that Yacub began to preach at the age of sixteen. He began to preach all over Arabia in the East. He preached among the thirty percent who were dissatisfied and got many of them to follow him. As they began to listen to Yacub's teachings and believe them, his teachings spread, his followers grew, and it created confusion in the land. So The Honorable Elijah Muhammad says that so much confusion came into existence over there that they threw Yacub's followers in jail, and as fast as they would throw them in jail they taught more people. So the teachings spread in jail. Finally Yacub was put in jail, under an alias. And one day, The Honorable Elijah Muhammad says, the thing began to get out of hand and the authorities went to the king and told him that they couldn't control these people, but that they had the leader of the people in jail right now, and the king said, "Take me to him."

And when the king went to the jail where Yacub was, he greeted Yacub with "As-Salaam-Alaikum, Mr. Yacub"—I know you're Mr. Yacub—and Yacub said, "Wa-Alaikum-Salaam"—I am Yacub! And the king said, "Look, I came to make an agreement with you. I know that you are the one that it is written or predicted would be on the scene in this day and would create a new race, and there is nothing we can do to stop you. But in order for us to have peace we want to make an agreement with you. In order to stop the confusion and for there to be some peace in the land, we want you to agree to take all who will follow you and exile yourselves out on an island in the Aegean Sea."

Yacub told them, "I'll go. But you've got to give me everything that I will need to bring into existence a new civilization. You've got to give me everything I'll need. You've got to supply me with everything I need for the next twenty years." And The Honorable Elijah Muhammad says that the king agreed with Yacub, the government of that day agreed to supply Yacub and his followers with everything they needed for twenty years. And he says that he gets this from the Bible where it says Jacob wrestled with the angel. Jacob was Yacub, and the angel that Jacob wrestled with wasn't God, it was the government of that day. "Angel" only means "a power," or somebody with power. When a man has his wings clipped, you say that he has lost his power, lost his position. So wings only mean a position of power entrapped him. So when it says Jacob wrestled with an angel, "angel" is only used as a symbol to hide the one he was really wrestling with. Jacob was wrestling with the government of that day. He made the government of that day give him everything he needed to last him and his followers for twenty years, just like The Honorable Elijah Muhammad is telling the government of this day that they've got to give us everything that we need in our own separate territory to last us for twenty to twenty-five years. You say, well, The Honorable Elijah Muhammad teaches us that Yacub agreed, the government agreed, Yacub took all of his followers down to the sea. The Honorable Elijah Muhammad says that Yacub took 59,999 of his followers down to the seaside, with himself making 60,000. He piled them in boats and took them out to an island in the Aegean Sea called Pelan. In the Bible it's called Patmos. When you read in the Book of Revelation where John, on the island of Patmos, heard the word of the Lord, that is Yacub. What was John doing on the island of Patmos? John was Yacub. John was out there getting ready to make a new race, he said, for the word of the Lord. What was the word of the Lord? The word was that in the year 8400 a new man would be made, a new race would be made. And when Yacub and his followers got out there his followers realized that Yacub was wiser than any man of his day, and they recognized him as a god; he was a god to them. So when you get to the place in the Bible where it says, "And God said, 'Let us make man,'" that was Yacub too, not the Supreme Being. It wasn't the Supreme Being who made the sun who said, "Let us make man." When the Supreme Being made the sun he said, "Let there be light." He said He was supreme, He was independent, He needed no help, no associates. But when it came to making a man, that god said, "Let us make man." He didn't speak with independence, because there were two different gods. God the Supreme Being made the light. His word is "be"; that's how He makes things. But Yacub, who was a lesser god, said to 59,999 of his followers, "Let us make man, let us make a man in our image, in our likeness. We're going to make a white man." It was Yacub talking: "Make him in our image and in our likeness, and give him dominion over the fowl of the air and the fish of the sea and the creatures of the land. And we'll call him Adam." It's only a name for the white man. The white man has taken mastery over the air, his airplanes rule the sky, his submarines and ships rule the sea, his armies rule the land. This was the man that was made six thousand years ago and the purpose for making him was so he could rule the world for six thousand years. That's the white man.

The Honorable Elijah Muhammad says that first thing Yacub did was to get his ministers, doctors, nurses, and cremators together. He gave them the laws because he had to set up a birth control law. He told the doctors whenever two black ones come to him to get married to stick a needle in their veins, take some blood, and go back and tell them that their blood doesn't match so that they can't marry. He also said when a black one and a brown one come, let them get married, or if two brown ones come let them get married. Then he told the nurse nine months after they're married, when you're ready to deliver their child, if it's a black child, put a needle in its brain and feed it to a wild animal or give it to the cremator. Let it be destroyed. But if it's a brown child, take that child to the mother and tell her that this is going to be a great man when he grows up because he's lighter than the others. Tell her that the child you destroyed was an angel baby and it went up to heaven to prepare a place for her when she dies. Same old lie they tell you today—when a little baby dies they tell you it went to heaven. When a baby dies he goes to the same place a man goes when he dies—right down into the ground. Is that right or wrong? So The Honorable Elijah Muhammad has taught us that Yacub right there set up his birth control law. Within two hundred years they had killed off all of the black babies on the island. Everything black on the island had been destroyed. And then Yacub only lived 150 years. But he left laws and rules and regulations behind, for his followers to go by. And after they had destroyed all of the black on the island of Pelan, they began to work on the brown germ. They saved the yellow and destroyed the brown, because you see in the black there's brown and in the brown there's yellow. Can you see how it goes? The darkest one always has a lighter one in it. So in the black man there's a brown man, in the brown man there's a yellow man, in the yellow man there's what? A white man. Oh yes. Getting weaker all the time. So it took two hundred years to destroy the black. And then they worked on the brown for two hundred years. And in two hundred years all the brown was destroyed and all they had on the island of Pelan was a yellow or mulatto-looking civilization. And then they went to work on it and began to destroy it. So that after six hundred years of destruction on the island of Pelan, they had grafted away the black, grafted away the brown, grafted away the yellow, so that all they had left was a pale-skinned, blue-eyed, blond-haired thing that you call a man. But actually the Bible calls him the devil. That's the devil that the Bible is talking about: old Lucifer, Satan, or the serpent. Because the lighter they got, the weaker they got. As they began to get lighter and lighter they grew weaker and weaker. Their blood became weaker, their bones became weaker, their minds became weaker, their morals became weaker. They became a wicked race; by nature wicked. Why by nature?

The Book says concerning the devil: "He was conceived in inequity and born in sin." What does this mean? At the outset the nurses had to kill the little black babies, but after a while it got so that the mother, having been brainwashed, hated that black one so much she killed it herself. Killed it herself, and saved the light one. And right on down for six hundred years. In order for the white one to come into existence, the darker one was always murdered, murdered, MURDERED! This went right into the nature of the child that was being born. The mother wanted a light baby when the child was being conceived. This went right into the baby. The mother hated black when the child was being conceived. This went right into the baby. So that at the end of the six hundred years, after planting the seed of inequity right into the brain, right into the mind, right into the heart, right into the nature of these people, by the time they got the white man, they had someone who by nature hated everything that was darker than he was. Why, they had to murder off the black to get to the brown. They had to murder off the brown in order to get to the yellow. They had to murder off the black, brown, and yellow in order to get to the white. And right to this very day the white man *by nature* wants to murder off the black, brown, and yellow. You don't have to teach him to kill the black man. He does it for sport. He does it for kicks. He does it because it's his nature to do it. Do you understand that?

So in six hundred years now they got a devil on the scene, a blue-eyed devil, blond-haired. Oh yes, they were out here on the island of Pelan. Yacub was dead. Yacub was their father but he never saw them. They never saw him. Yacub was their god. When the Bible says no man had seen God, that's what it means. No white man has seen their god. None of them saw Yacub because Yacub only lived to be 150 years old. This doesn't mean that no man can see God the Supreme Being. Why, the Book of Revelation says when He comes every eye will see Him. So The Honorable Elijah Muhammad says after these devils got grafted—now we're not going to call them white any more. We call them what they are. White, that's their color, but devil, that's what they are. These aren't white people. You're not using the right language when you say the white man. You call it the devil. When you call him devil you're calling him by his name, and he's got another name—Satan; another name—serpent; another name—snake; another name—beast. All these names are in the Bible for the white man. Another name—Pharaoh; another name—Caesar; another name—France; French; Frenchman; Englishman; American; all those are just names for the devil.

So after they were out there six hundred years, after

they were made and grafted and Yacub was dead, then they packed up their bags and made it back to civilization. Yacub had left them some laws to go by. He left them a science called "tricknology": how to divide and conquer. Yacub told these people in his book: "All you got to do to take over the world is lie. Go back among the black people. Take your woman and send her to the black man's woman and let her lie about the neighbor across the street. And then send another woman to that woman to lie on this woman to that woman. And when they get through spreading those lies and they all start fighting and killing one another, you tell them to let you be the mediator." This is the trick the white man used. It all comes from Yacub. You see, he's an underdog. He's a minority, and the only way a minority can rule a majority is to *divide* the majority. This is the trick that the white man was born to execute among dark mankind here on this Earth. Yacub said, "When you go back among them, lie about them to each other, and when they start fighting, ask them to let you be the mediator. And as soon as you become the mediator then you're the boss." The white man has done this trick everywhere. Here in America to the Indians. He sent one priest to the Indians in New York and another priest to the Indians in Pennsylvania and both of them would tell lies to both Indians, and the Indians who had never been at war with each other would start beating the tom-toms, the war drums, and then as they got ready to fight the priest would run in and say, "Let me be the mediator."

So he told the New York Indians, you just move out to Minnesota; and the Pennsylvania Indians, you move out to Oklahoma. That would leave the whole states of New York and Pennsylvania for the white man. You see how he does it? He's all over the world. He's a mediator. He's an instigator and a mediator. He instigates division and dissension and as soon as they start fighting one another he says, "OK, I'll settle it." If you don't think so look all over the world right now. Every place on this earth you have a division: South Korea–North Korea, South Vietnam–North Vietnam. Right or wrong? He is the one that makes this decision. He doesn't let anybody get together, but when it comes to his kind he's united. United States means all white people are united. United States of Europe, or European Common Market—they want to get together. But when you start talking about a United States of Asia, or a United States of Africa, why he says, "Oh no, too many different languages [chuckle]. You all don't have anything in common." You see how he does it? He always discourages unity among others but he encourages unity among his own kind. "United We Stand," that doesn't mean *you*. That means the white man. The white man is the one who stands united.

So The Honorable Elijah Muhammad says that these devils went back into Arabia. When they got there they started telling lies, started confusion, and in six months' time they had turned heaven into hell. Oh yeah, they had so much fighting going on among our people, brother, it became hell. We never did fight each other; we loved each other, we were in harmony with each other. And when these devils came back into our midst they turned our paradise into a hell. So it was taken to the king and the king looked into the book and said, "Why, these are Yacub's people." He said, "They were made to do what they're doing and the only way to have peace is to get rid of all of them. Put them all to death." So the king gave the order for all of the devils to be rounded up. And by devils I mean all those blue-eyed, blond-haired, white things. He gave orders for them to be rounded up there in the East, and they were rounded up. They were rounded up and taken down to the edge of the Arabian Desert. They were stripped naked, stripped of everything except their language. The Honorable Elijah Muhammad says that we put lambskin aprons around their waists to hide their nakedness. We put them in chains and marched them across the hot sands of the Arabian Desert. This is what the black man did to the white man, brothers. This is what the gods did to the devils. Actually, if you think I don't know what I'm talking about, those of you who are Masons, you go through this and don't understand it. When you go in, they put a lambskin apron around your waist. They put you in what's called the "cable tow." Right or wrong? And then they make you jump up and down on an electric mat. Make you take off your shoes and put the juice in the mat and make you jump up and down. Why? What are they getting at? That's all a sign of what happened to the white man six thousand years ago. It just doesn't have anything to do with you, but you're supposed to be walking on hot sands when you jump up and down. Right or wrong? You've all been in some of that stuff. They tell you that's crossing the hot sand. And if you walk up to a Negro Mason and you ask him, "When you crossed the hot sand were you walking or riding?" he'll say, "I was walking." He's a fool. Because he was riding. He was riding horseback. He was riding on a camel. It was the white man that was in chains. It was the white man that had the apron around him. It was the white man that was walking the white sand. We walked them at high noon. We wouldn't even let them walk at night. We stopped at night. And you know how hot the sun and the sands are in Arabia. We expected the white man to die when we were running him out of the East. But that fool lived, brother [chuckle]. He lived. A lot of them died on the desert. And I might come back—all of this is tied up in the Masonic ritual. When a man gets initiated into the higher degrees of that order he goes through this. They put on the chains, they put on the aprons, and they darken him up and pretend to be driving him across. Then when he gets up to the top order in those degrees, they tell him what it means. The white man, they tell the white man what it means: a white Shriner, a white Mason, what it means. A Negro never learns what it means. But it actually points back toward the time when the white man, who is the devil, or Adam, as they say, was cast out of the Garden. When the Bible says Adam sinned and was cast out of the Garden, this is what is meant. And an angel was put at the East gate to keep him from coming back in. When the white man was run out of the East by the Muslims six thousand years ago into the caves of Europe, the people called Turks were put there at the Straits of the Dardanelles, with swords, and any old devil that they caught trying to come back across the water—WHOP!!! —off went his head. The Book tells you that the angel had a flaming sword, and any time any of them tried to come back across they were put to death.

The Honorable Elijah Muhammad says that the white man went down into the caves of Europe and he lived there for two thousand years on all fours. Within one thousand years after he had gotten there he was on all fours, couldn't stand upright. You watch an old cracker today. Crackers don't walk upright like black people do. Every time you look at them, they're about to go down on all fours. But those who have had some education, they straighten up a little bit because they're taught how to straighten up. But a black man can be the most dumb, illiterate thing you can find anywhere, and he still walks like a million dollars because by nature he's upright, by nature he stands up. But a white man has to be stood up. You have to put a white man on the square. But the black is born on the square.

Can we prove it? Yes. You notice in the East, dark people carry things on their heads, don't they? Just throw it up there and walk with it, showing you they have perfect poise, perfect balance. It just comes natural to them. You and I lost our poise. We, you, can't even wear a hat on your head, hardly, today [chuckle]. The Honorable Elijah Muhammad says that within one thousand years after the white people were up in the caves they were on all fours. And they were living in the outdoors where it's cold, just as cold over there as it is outside right now. They didn't have clothes. So by being out there in the cold their hair got longer and longer. Hair grew all over their bodies. By being on all fours, the end of their spine begin to grow. They grew a little tail that came out from the end of their spine . . . Oh yes, this was the white man, brother, up in the caves of Europe. He had a tail that long. You ever notice that anything that walks on all fours has a tail? That which straightens up doesn't have a tail, because when you get down, you see, you just make that spine come right on out. And just like a dog, he was crawling around up there. He was hairy as a dog. He had a tail like a dog. He had a smell like a dog. And nothing could get along with him but another dog. The Honorable Elijah Muhammad says that all the beasts up in Europe wanted to kill the white man. Yeah, they tried to kill the white man. They were after the white man. They hated the white man. So, he says, what the white man would do, he'd dig a hole in the hill, that was his cave. And his mother and his daughter and his wife would all be in there with the dog. The only thing that made friends with the white man was the dog. Everything else hated him. He'd sit outside of the cave at night in a tree with rocks in his hand, and if any beast came up and tried to get in the cave at his family, he'd throw rocks at it, or he'd have a club that he'd swing down and try to drive it away with it. But the dog stayed in the cave with his family. It was then that the dog and the white man amalgamated. The white woman went with the dog while they were living in the caves of Europe. And right to this very day the white woman will tell you there is nothing she loves better than a dog. They tell you that a dog is a man's best friend. A dog isn't a black man's best friend. God is the black man's best friend. But a dog is the white man's best friend. They lived in that cave with those dogs and right now they got that dog smell. They got that dog . . . They are dog lovers. A dog can get in a white man's house and eat at his table, lick out of his plate. They'll kiss the dog right on the nose and think nothing of it. You're not a dog kisser. You don't see black people kissing or rubbing noses with dogs. But little white children will hug dogs and kiss dogs and *eat* with dogs. Am I right or wrong? You-all have been inside their kitchens cooking their food, and making their beds, you *know* how they live. The dog will live right in the white man's house, better than you can; you try and break your way in there and they'll put a rope around your neck [chuckle], but the dog has got free run of the whole house. He's the white man's best friend.

The Honorable Elijah Muhammad says that they lived up there for two thousand years, and at the end of two thousand years the scientists in the East, realizing that it was originally predestined that the white race would rule for six thousand years, and that they had already lost two thousand years in the caves of Europe, sent a prophet up there, from Mecca, to teach the white race, the race of devils, how to become civilized again, and become upright, and come back and rule the way they had originally been meant to. The name of that prophet was Moses. Moses never went down into Egypt. Moses went into the caves of Europe and civilized the white man. It was Moses who raised the devil from a dead level to a perpendicular and placed him on the square. Moses taught the white man how to cook his food. Moses taught the white man how to build a house for himself. He taught the white man also some of the tricknology that Yacub had originally meant for him, and it was Moses who put the white man back on the road toward civilization. He told him that he was supposed to rule for six thousand years, but that much of the time had already been lost, and at the end of time one would come who would destroy the whole white race. Moses taught them this. And this is why when the Jews, two thousand years later, were looking for the Messiah, they thought that Jesus was the Messiah and they put him to death because they knew when the Messiah came he was going to destroy that whole race of devils. The Jews knew this, so they put him to death thinking that they could stop him from destroying them. But actually, they made a mistake because Jesus two thousand years ago wasn't the Messiah. Their time wasn't up two thousand years ago. Their time would not be up until two thousand years later, the day and time that we're living in right now.

So, brothers and sisters, my time has expired. I just wanted to point out that the white man, a race of devils, was made six thousand years ago. This doesn't mean to tell you that this implies any kind of hate. They're just a race of devils. They were made six thousand years ago,

they were made to rule for six thousand years, and their
time expired in the year 1914. The only reason God didn't
remove them then was because you and I were here in
their clutches and God gave them an extension of time—
not *them* an extension of time, but they received an extension of time to give the wise men of the East the opportunity to get into this House of Bondage and "awaken"
the Lost Sheep. Once the American so-called Negroes have
been awakened to a knowledge of themselves and of their
own God and of the white man, then they're on their own.
Then it'll be left up to you and me whether we want to
integrate into this wicked race or leave them and separate
and go to our own. And if we integrate we'll be destroyed
along with them. If we separate then we have a chance
for salvation. So on that note, in the name of Allah, and
His Messenger The Honorable Elijah Muhammad, I bring
my talk to a close, "As-Salaam-Alaikum."

With your hands outstretched in this manner, follow
silently in the closing Muslim prayer:
In the name of Allah, the Beneficent, the Merciful,
All praise is due to Allah, the Lord of the Worlds,
The Beneficent, the Merciful,
Master of this Day of Judgment in which we now live,
Thee do we serve and Thee do we beseech for thine aid.
Guide us on the right path,
The path upon which Thou hast bestowed favors,
Not the path upon which Thy wrath is brought down
Nor of those who go astray after they have heard Thy
      teaching.
Say: He Allah is one God
Allah is He upon whom nothing is independent but
Upon whom we all depend.

He neither begets nor is He begotten and none is like Him.
I bear witness there is none to be served but Allah,
And I bear witness that The Honorable Elijah Muhammad is
    mad is
His True Servant and Last Apostle . . . Amen

The Black Revolution

MALCOLM X: Dr. Powell, distinguished guests, brothers and sisters, friends, and even our enemies. As a follower and minister of The Honorable Elijah Muhammad, who is the Messenger of Allah to the American so-called Negro, I am very happy to accept Dr. Powell's invitation to be here this evening at the Abyssinian Baptist Church and to express or at least to try to represent The Honorable Elijah Muhammad's views on this most timely topic, the black revolution.

First, however, there are some questions we have to put to you. Since the black masses here in America are now in open revolt against the American system of segregation, will these same black masses turn toward integration or will they turn toward complete separation? Will these awakened black masses demand integration into the white society that enslaved them or will they demand complete separation from that cruel white society that has enslaved them? Will the exploited and oppressed black masses seek integration with their white exploiters and white oppressors or will these awakened black masses truly revolt and separate themselves completely from this wicked race that has enslaved us?

These are just some quick questions that I think will provoke some thoughts in your minds and my mind. How can the so-called Negroes who call themselves enlightened leaders expect the poor black sheep to integrate into a society of bloodthirsty white wolves, white wolves who have already been sucking on our blood for over four hundred years here in America? Or will these black sheep also revolt against the "false shepherd," the handpicked Uncle Tom Negro leader, and seek complete separation so that we can escape from the den of the wolves rather than be integrated with wolves in this wolves' den? And since we are in church and most of us here profess to believe in God, there is another question: When the "good shepherd" comes will he integrate his long-lost sheep with white wolves? According to the Bible when God comes he won't even let his sheep integrate with goats. And if his sheep can't be safely integrated with goats they certainly aren't safe integrated with wolves. The Honorable Elijah Muhammad teaches us that no people on earth fit the Bible's symbolic picture about the Lost Sheep more so than America's twenty million so-called Negroes and there has never in history been a more vicious and bloodthirsty wolf than the American white man. He teaches us that for four hundred years America has been nothing but a wolves' den for twenty million so-called Negroes, twenty million second-class citizens, and this black revolution that is developing against the white wolf today is developing because The Honorable Elijah Muhammad, a godsent shepherd, has opened the eyes of our people. And the black masses can now see that we have all been here in this white doghouse long, too long. The black masses don't want segregation nor do we want integration. What we want is complete separation. In short, we don't want to be segregated by the white man, we don't want to be integrated with the white man, we want to be separated from the white man. And now our religious leader and teacher, The Honorable Elijah Muhammad, teaches us that this is the only intelligent and lasting solution to the present race problem. In order to fully understand why the Muslim followers of The Honorable Elijah Muhammad actually reject hypocritical promises of integration it must first be understood by everyone that we are a religious group, and as a religious group we can in no way be equated or compared to the nonreligious civil rights groups. We are Muslims because we believe in Allah. We are Muslims because we practice the religion of Islam. The Honorable Elijah Muhammad teaches us that there is but one God, the creator and sustainer of the entire universe, the all-wise, all-powerful Supreme Being. The great God whose proper name is Allah. The Honorable Elijah Muhammad also teaches us that Islam is an Arabic word that means "complete submission to the will of Allah or obedience to the God of truth, God of peace, the God of righteousness, the God whose proper name is Allah." And he teaches us that the word Muslim is used to describe one who submits to God, one who obeys God. In other words a Muslim is one who strives to live a life of righteousness. You may ask what does the religion of Islam have to do with the American so-called Negro's changing attitude toward himself, toward the white man, toward segregation, toward integration, and toward separation, and what part will this religion of Islam play in the current black revolution that is sweeping the American continent today? The Honorable Elijah Muhammad teaches us that Islam is the religion of naked truth, naked truth, undressed truth, truth that is not dressed up, and he says that truth is the only thing that will truly set our people free. Truth will open our eyes and enable us to see the white wolf as he really is. Truth will stand us on our own feet. Truth will make us walk for ourselves instead of leaning on others who mean our people no good. Truth not only shows us who our real enemy is, truth also gives us the strength and the know-how to separate ourselves from that enemy. Only a blind man will walk into the open embrace of his enemy, and only a blind people, a people who are blind to the truth about their enemies, will seek to embrace or integrate with that enemy. Why, Jesus himself prophesied. You shall know the truth and it shall make you free. Beloved brothers and sisters, Jesus never said that Abraham Lincoln would make us free. He never said that the Congress would make us free. He never said that the Senate or Supreme Court or John Kennedy would make us free. Jesus two thousand years ago looked down the wheel of time and saw your and my plight here today and he knew the tricky high court, Supreme Court, desegregation decisions would only lull you into a deeper sleep, and the tricky promises of the hypocritical politicians on civil rights legislation would only be designed to advance you and me from ancient slavery to modern slavery. But Jesus did prophesy that when Elijah comes in the spirit and power of truth he said that Elijah would teach you the truth. Elijah would guide you with truth and Elijah would protect you with truth and make you free indeed. And brothers and sisters, that Elijah, the one whom Jesus has said was to come, has come and is in America today in the person of The Honorable Elijah Muhammad.

This Elijah, the one whom they said was to come and

who has come, teaches those of us who are Muslims that our white slave masters have always known the truth and they have always known that truth alone would set us free. Therefore this same American white man kept the truth hidden from our people. He kept us in the darkness of ignorance. He made us spiritually blind by depriving us of the light of truth. During the four hundred years that we have spent confined to the darkness of ignorance here in this land of bondage, our American enslavers have given us an overdose of their own white-controlled Christian religion, but have kept all other religions hidden from us, especially the religion of Islam. And for this reason, Almighty God Allah, the God of our forefathers, has raised The Honorable Elijah Muhammad from the midst of our downtrodden people here in America. And this same God has missioned The Honorable Elijah Muhammad to spread the naked truth to America's twenty million so-called Negroes, and the truth alone will make you and me free.

The Honorable Elijah Muhammad teaches us that there is but one God whose proper name is Allah, and one religion, the religion of Islam, and that this one God will not rest until he has used his religion to establish one world—a universal, one-world brotherhood. But in order to set up his righteous world God must first bring down this wicked white world. The black revolution against the injustices of the white world is all part of God's divine plan. God must destroy the world of slavery and evil in order to establish a world based upon freedom, justice, and equality. The followers of The Honorable Elijah Muhammad religiously believe that we are living at the end of this wicked world, the world of colonialism, the world of slavery, the end of the Western world, the white world or the Christian world, or the end of the wicked white man's Western world of Christianity.

The Honorable Elijah Muhammad teaches us that the symbolic stories in all religious scriptures paint a prophetic picture of today. He says that the Egyptian House of Bondage was only a prophetic picture of America. Mighty Babylon was only a prophetic picture of America. The wicked cities of Sodom and Gomorrah painted only a prophetic picture of America. No one here in this church tonight can deny that America is the mightiest government on earth today, the mightiest, the richest, and the wickedest. And no one in this church tonight dare deny that America's wealth and power stemmed from 310 years of slave labor contributed from the American so-called Negro.

The Honorable Elijah Muhammad teaches us that these same so-called American Negroes are God's long-lost people who are symbolically described in the Bible as the Lost Sheep or the Lost Tribe of Israel. We who are Muslims believe in God, we believe in his scriptures, we believe in prophecy. Nowhere in the scriptures did God ever integrate his enslaved people with their slave masters. God always separates his oppressed people from their oppressor and then destroys the oppressor. God has never deviated from his divine pattern in the past and The Honorable Elijah Muhammad says that God will not deviate from that divine pattern today. Just as God destroyed the enslavers in the past, God is going to destroy this wicked white enslaver of our people here in America.

God wants us to separate ourselves from this wicked white race here in America because this American House of Bondage is number one on God's list for divine destruction today. I repeat: This American House of Bondage is number one on God's list for divine destruction today. He warns us to remember Noah never taught integration, Noah taught separation; Moses never taught integration,

Moses taught separation. The innocent must always be given a chance to separate themselves from the guilty before the guilty are executed. No one is more innocent than the poor, blind, American so-called Negro who has been led astray by blind Negro leaders, and no one on earth is more guilty than the blue-eyed white man who has used his control and influence over the Negro leader to lead the rest of our people astray.

Beloved brothers and sisters here, a beautiful here at the Abyssinian Baptist Church in Harlem, because of America's evil deeds against the so-called Negroes, like Egypt and Babylon before her, America herself now stands before the bar of justice. America herself is now facing her day of judgment, and she can't escape because God Himself is the judge. If America can't atone for the crimes she has committed against the twenty million so-called Negroes, if she can't undo the evils that she has brutally and mercilessly heaped upon our people these past four hundred years, The Honorable Elijah Muhammad says that America has signed her own doom. And you, our people, would be foolish to accept her deceitful offers of integration at this late date into her doomed society.

Can America escape? Can America atone? And if so how can she atone for these crimes? In my conclusion I must point out that The Honorable Elijah Muhammad says a desegregated theater, a desegregated lunch counter won't solve our problem. Better jobs won't solve our problems. An integrated cup of coffee isn't sufficient pay for four hundred years of slave labor. He also says that a better job, a better job in the white man's factory, or a better job in the white man's business, or a better job in the white man's industry or economy is, at best, only a temporary solution. He says that the only lasting and permanent solution is complete separation on some land that we can call our own. Therefore, The Honorable Elijah Muhammad says that this problem can be solved and solved forever just by sending our people back to our own homeland or back to our own people, but that this government should provide the transportation plus everything else we need to get started again in our own country. This government should give us everything we need in the form of machinery, material, and finance—enough to last for twenty to twenty-five years until we can become an independent people and an independent nation in our own land. He says that if the American government is afraid to send us back to our own country and to our own people, then America should set aside some separated territory right here in the Western hemisphere where the two races can live apart from each other, since we certainly don't get along peacefully while we are together.

The Honorable Elijah Muhammad says that the size of the territory can be judged according to our population. If a seventh of the population of this country is black, then give us a seventh of the territory, a seventh part of the country. And that is not asking too much because we already worked for the man for four hundred years.

He says it must not be in the desert, but where there is plenty of rain and much mineral wealth. We want fertile, productive land on which we can farm and provide our own people with food, clothing, and shelter. He says that this government should supply us on that territory with the machinery and other tools needed to dig into the earth. Give us everything we need for twenty to twenty-five years until we can produce and supply our own needs.

And in my conclusion I repeat: We want no part of integration with this wicked race that enslaved us. We want complete separation from this wicked race of devils. But he also says we should not be expected to leave America empty-handed. After four hundred years of slave labor, we have some back pay coming. A bill that is owed to us and must be collected. If the government of America truly repents of its sins against our people and atones by giving us our true share of the land and the wealth, then America can save herself. But if America waits for God to step in and force her to make a just settlement, God will take this entire continent away from the white man. And the Bible says that God can then give the kingdom to whomsoever he pleases. I thank you.

Questions and Answers

POWELL: Please distinguish between segregation and separation.

MALCOLM X: Yes, sir. The Honorable Elijah Muhammad teaches us that segregation is that which is done to inferiors by superiors. Separation is done voluntarily by two people. An example: You'll notice an Oriental community like Chinatown is never called a segregated community, but the so-called Negro community is always called a segregated community. The reason Chinatown is not regarded as a segregated community is that Chinese in Chinatown control all their own businesses, all their own banks, their own politics, their own everything, whereas in the so-called Negro community everything is controlled by outsiders. We live in a regulated or segregated community. We are not for segregation but we are for separation. When you are segregated that is done to you by someone else; when you are separated you do that to yourself.

POWELL: What do you think of the black man who is not a Moslem, but who is part of the black revolution?

MALCOLM X: The Honorable Elijah Muhammad teaches us that all black people by nature and birth are Muslims by nature, but they don't know it! So he teaches us that every one of the twenty million black people in this country are actually Muslims. They are asleep now, but when they wake up they'll all be Muslims.

POWELL: Here is one from the members of the Abyssinian Church: "My present preacher is in front of a cross which was given him by his Imperial Majesty, Haile Selassie, and he says that the country of Ethiopia was Christian before Islam or Muslims were founded." How do you feel about this?

MALCOLM X: This is actually incorrect. Those of you who are students of theology, if you take the time to look into the Koran, it points out in there that the Muslims regard Jesus as a Muslim and Moses as a Muslim and Abraham as a Muslim. In fact our own Scriptures teach us that all of the prophets were Muslims, Muslim only being one who believes in God. So the religion that was taught by Jesus in that geographical area of this earth two thousand years ago was the religion of Islam. This is why I say all of us are Muslims. But here in America you call yourselves Christians which comes from a Greek word and Jesus wasn't a Greek! If you go and find him and ask him what he was, he'll tell you he was a Muslim too!

POWELL: If what you said tonight came true and we had one-seventh of the land, would conditions among black men governing their own area be any better than among the white man?

MALCOLM X: They couldn't be worse!

POWELL: Here is one from Kenya: "I agree one hundred percent that the so-called Negroes have a right to go back to Africa. If they went back would they be willing to follow our African way of life?"

MALCOLM X: I was in Africa in 1959, thanks to The Honorable Elijah Muhammad, and while there I noticed that the so-called Negroes from here who went back tried to act American, which means they tried to act white. They never identified with the African. They didn't think of themselves as being black or the same as the people in whose midst they were, and because they didn't identify with the African the African couldn't identify with them. But by me being a Muslim, having been taught by The Honorable Elijah Muhammad, I'm black first, America doesn't even come into my mind. I don't think of myself as an American so I don't try to act like one. Which means they don't mistake me for a white man. But as a Muslim, when we go back among Africans, our feelings are the same as the Africans'; our objectives are the same as the Africans'. We are one people, so we get along well with each other. Usually the only so-called American Negroes whom the Africans see are the ones that have been sent over by the State Department, Uncle Toms, stool pigeons . . .

POWELL: Why do you, as a Muslim leader, come to speak in a Christian church?

MALCOLM X: We who follow The Honorable Elijah Muhammad accept invitations from whoever gives us one. We take advantage of every opportunity to let the world know what The Honorable Elijah Muhammad is teaching our people and doing for our people. And we thank the Abyssinian Baptist Church, along with Dr. Powell and everybody in this neighborhood, for this invitation tonight. As he said a moment ago, I doubt if you could have this type of forum in any other church, because most of these other Negro churches are scared.

POWELL: I have a question of my own: Would you invite me to speak in one of your temples?

MALCOLM X: A good question. We are having a mass rally at 116th Street and Lenox Avenue this coming Sat-

urday. Probably it will be the largest group of black people that you have ever seen come together anywhere at
any time, and we invite Congressman Powell to come out
there and speak on Saturday, and come out and speak at
the Mosque on Sunday.

POWELL: I have a handful of questions and I'm trying
to pick out those that are most important. You ask that one-
seventh of the country be given over to the black man for
a period of twenty-five years. What would we do at the
end of twenty-five years?

MALCOLM X: I didn't say for a period of twenty-five
years. If you notice the press usually paints the picture
that Mr. Muhammad is asking for part of this country.
That is not the case. His first solution is for the government to let us go back home to our own people. But we
shouldn't go back broke. Part of this economy belongs to
us. That gold in Fort Knox and that silver down in Philadelphia does not belong to the white man. That is for
wages that they never paid our people for four hundred
years. So he says that the government should let us go
back, but not empty-handed. Now if the government
doesn't want us to go back, then give us part of this country. And he says this part can be determined by the number of our own people. If our people make up a seventh,
or a tenth, or a quarter of the population then give us a
quarter of the country, or a seventh of the country, or
whatever amount that's necessary. But when we go into
our territory he says that the government should provide
us with everything we need. Pay us! You send billions of
dollars to Latin America, Poland and Yugoslavia, and
India and they have never been a slave here and have
made no contribution to this economy. If you send billions
of dollars abroad give something to your ex-slaves who
have been more faithful than they.

POWELL: You claim to follow Islam. How can you make this claim when the Prophet Muhammad, being the founder of this dynasty, invited all nations and all people to follow the religion and when you are aiming your particular religion, Muslim movement, only at black people? Is there a contradiction?

MALCOLM X: No. Number one, Muhammad was in Arabia fourteen hundred years ago and he taught that all men are brothers. If you notice, the spread of that religion of brotherhood went rapidly in Asia and Africa where the dark people of this earth believed by nature in being hospitable, friendly, and brotherly toward everyone. But when that religion of brotherhood reached Europe it ran into a stone wall, because the white man by nature cannot practice brotherhood even with another white man. And so The Honorable Elijah Muhammad teaches us that Islam is a religious prescription that God has given him to heal the sin-sick so-called Negroes in America. And you and I are in such bad shape we don't need to waste any time talking to anybody else. We need to bring you right into the emergency ward and give you first preference.

POWELL: Would you allow white people to join the Black Muslim group?

MALCOLM X: No. Let them start their own. That's what's the matter with our people. Too many whites have joined us.

POWELL: Do you hate the white man?

MALCOLM X: We don't even think about him. How can anybody ask us do we hate the man who kidnapped us four hundred years ago, brought us here and stripped us of our history, stripped us of our culture, stripped us of our language, stripped us of everything that you could use today to prove that you were ever part of the human family, brought you down to the level of an animal, sold you from plantation to plantation like a sack of wheat, sold you like a sack of potatoes, sold you like a horse and a cow, and then hung you up from one end of the country to the other, and then you ask me do I hate him? Why, your question is worthless!

POWELL: If you advocate separation why do you ask the white man to finance your separation?

MALCOLM X: As I pointed out during the brief lecture, we aren't asking the white man to finance anything. I might answer in this way. Each individual here is poor, and individually you are a poor person; but if someone were able to collect all of the wages of the people in this church at the end of the week, they would have a lot of money collected. And if they could collect the wages of just these people in here for a year they'd be rich. When you see that, think how rich America had to become collecting the wages not of just a handful of people but of millions of black people working not for a year but for 310 years, without one day's pay. And it is your labor that made America rich, and it is the blood that you sacrificed on foreign battlefields that made America powerful. So when we say, when The Honorable Elijah Muhammad says to America, give us our cut, give us our share, give us what belongs to us, it is not a case of asking America to finance us. No, we want our share of what we invested here. And if we get it then America has salvation, but if she doesn't pay off her debt God will collect and God won't take part payment. He will take the entire country . . . and give it to whom he pleases.

The Old Negro
and the New Negro

*In 1963, with Malcolm X already a national figure and
the Muslim cause for which he was the most articulate
spokesman clearly gaining ground among the black masses
of America,* The Saturday Evening Post *published an
article entitled "Merchants of Hate." It was nothing very
new for Malcolm or the Muslims. Four years before there
had been a major television program aired about the
Muslims called "The Hate That Hate Produced," and
during the intervening years the "hate" image had been
promulgated by virtually all the major newspapers and
magazines of the country. One of the most frequently asked
questions that Malcolm had to confront in those days was:
"Mr. Malcolm X, why do you teach black supremacy, and
hate?" That question, or its many variants, Malcolm relates, was like a red flag being waved in front of him.
But he learned to field it with characteristic wit, such as
the example he cites in his autobiography: "For the white
man to ask the black man if he hates him is just like the*

rapist asking the raped, *or the wolf asking the* sheep, '*Do you hate me?' The white man is in no moral position to accuse anyone else of hate!"*

It is to this article, "Merchants of Hate," that Malcolm refers several times in the following speech-interview.

MALCOLM X: With regard to *The Saturday Evening Post* article, it's just about what you would expect from a nationally circulated magazine that is writing about a group of black people not under the influence or control of the white man. To me the magazine article was, by and large, a great deal of propaganda. The very fact that it is named "Merchants of Hate" gives a clue to the purpose or objective that the people who were responsible for the article had in mind. I think that the white man has a great deal of nerve to refer to any black people as merchants of hate in the face of the hell that black people have caught in this country at the hands of the white man, even at a time when the whites are admitting that they have brutalized black people for four hundred years. They kidnapped us and brought us here; they deprived us of our rights; they made us slaves; they sold our people from one plantation to another, from one auction block to another. And even right now, 1963, they have to confess they are still depriving the black people here in America, not only of civil rights but even of human rights. And behind all of this mistreatment and abuse that whites have inflicted upon the black people in this country, again I say, I think that a white man in a magazine published by white people has a whole lot of nerve charging black people with teaching some kind of hate about them. If black people in this country behind the deeds they have experienced at the hands of the white man don't hate him because of what they have done to him, why a person would be wasting his time trying to teach someone hate behind that. The Honorable Elijah Muhammad doesn't teach hate, he teaches black people to love each other.

MODERATOR: Was there anything in that article, Malcolm X, relative to the Muslims that was true?

MALCOLM X: There could have been. I think when it says that The Honorable Elijah Muhammad teaches us to reform ourselves of the vices and evils of this society, drunkenness, dope addiction, how to work and provide a living for our family, take care of our children and our wives—when it pointed out these aspects it was speaking truth, but this is a thing that black people have to guard against. Oftentimes a propagandist who is shrewd will tell just enough truth to make you believe that he is being objective and to get you to listen and then he starts injecting the negative side, and this is where we become resentful.

MODERATOR: They did make some mention in the article, however, of the growing strength of the Black Muslims.

MALCOLM X: Not because they wanted to but because they had to. I think the white man has to face the fact that black people in this country are tired of sitting around waiting for the white man to make up his mind that we are human beings. Therefore, the type of so-called Negro leadership that represents this hat-in-hand, patient, wait-another-hundred-years approach, that type of leadership is losing its grip on the mind of the masses of people. So when a man like The Honorable Elijah Muhammad steps forth in the midst of the so-called Negroes and calls it just like it is, and shows the black people that we don't have to compromise with the white man because we are right—right is on our side—and when right is on your side, and when what a man is doing to you is wrong, you don't have to sit around and give him another hundred years to get his house in order. It is this type of approach that The Honorable Elijah Muhammad is using that makes the masses of black people see that he is the man for them. And it is also helping his growth.

MODERATOR: Mention was made in the article of the business prospects, of progress made by the Muslims, and in so doing accusations were made in the article that most of the businesses of the Black Muslims are very small neighborhood businesses. Is that true?

MALCOLM X: Well, sir, when the white man himself was starting out his businesses in this country they all started out as neighborhood businesses. Woolworth started out with one store and over the years he has developed a chain into a tremendous economic enterprise. Sears, Roebuck— all of your big chain businesses or your industries that the white man has today were started as small businesses. Any business that you can point out started out small, and this is where the Negro has made his mistake. He wants to start out right now exactly as the white man is. He doesn't realize that you have to start out small and develop into that which you ultimately will become. And The Honorable Elijah Muhammad has actually showed his business ingenuity by showing how to start out small and develop our businesses—make them grow—and then our business ability grows right along with that business. And there is nothing wrong with that. And also that article did point out the fact that most of the businesses aren't owned by the Nation of Islam or the Muslim group per se, but rather most of the businesses are owned by the individual Muslims, and this is true. The Honorable Elijah Muhammad encourages every so-called Negro that respects the religion of Islam to stand on his own two feet and start doing something for himself. So the money that we used to throw away when we were Christians—nightclubbing and drinking and smoking and participating in these other acts of immorality—the money that we save when we become Muslims—we channel it into these small business enterprises and try to develop them to where they can provide some job opportunities for the rest of our people. And I can cite a good example in New York where we have one particular brother who, when he was a Christian, was a drunkard. He was a mechanic. He used to work for the white man. And when he came to Muhammad's Mosque in New York he immediately stopped drinking and he started saving his money and he opened up a little two-by-four, or two-bit, garage in a store on 115th Street, and within three or four years he had saved up enough money to buy himself a home on Long Island plus expand his small business into a five-story garage, where he now employs fifty or so persons. Which means he is now in a position to create employment for Negroes. And he has done this only since becoming a Muslim. He is only an example of what The Honorable Elijah Muhammad has taught black men to do across the country. Instead of begging the white man for what he has, he says we should get together and start doing something for ourselves. As long as a lot of these Negroes want to continue to beg from the white man and sit around and wait for the crumbs to fall from the white man's table, they don't like what Mr. Muhammad is forcing them to do: stand on their own two feet. So they slip up to the white man and whisper in his ear and make the white man think—the gullible white man think—that The Honorable Elijah Muhammad is teaching hate and trying to develop some kind of an army to overthrow the white man. And as long as the white man listens to that type of Negro he will end up overthrowing himself.

MODERATOR: Malcolm, I understand that you were at

the Irvine Auditorium at the University of Pennsylvania today as a guest of the youth chapter of the NAACP and the report that I received was that you had better than three thousand people out there, with a number of people standing outside who were not able to gain entrance. Is that true?

MALCOLM X: That's correct.

MODERATOR: I am wondering what your subject was and what you talked about out there.

MALCOLM X: Well, before I tell you the subject I want to comment on that crowd. You'll find that this is a pattern that we run into across the country. Wherever a Muslim makes an appearance and gives a lecture, no matter what type of crowd comes out, even a capacity crowd, very seldom will you read too much about it in the press. Very seldom will you get any indication from the press that the people in that city or in that community or in that college or in that university are showing any genuine interest in what the Muslim has to say. But when an integrationist like King or someone else comes into the city, if he talks to five people this will be blown up in the press and it will be made to appear that this is the man who represents the black masses, and that all of the black masses endorse the type of peaceful-suffering, hat-in-hand, tongue-in-cheek doctrine that is usually displayed on those occasions. So basically one of the reasons why you never hear too much about occasions like this is because of that fact. Now, my subject today dealt with primarily two different Negroes: the old Negro and the new Negro.

MODERATOR: Will you tell us something about it?

MALCOLM X: I will. This is the thing that whites need to be made aware of, that there is an old Negro and a new Negro. The old Negro is the one that the white man is familiar with. The new Negro is the one that has resulted from the teachings of The Honorable Elijah Muhammad, and the whites in this country are not too familiar with this type. Back in slavery they also had two types, and to understand the types today you have to understand the two types that existed during slavery. During slavery, historians agree, there were what were known as the house Negro and the field Negro. The house Negro was the one who lived in the master's house, ate the master's food, at the master's table usually—after the master had finished with it. He dressed like the master, which means he wore the same type of clothing that the master did, but usually it was clothing handed down to him by the master. He identified the master's house as his own. If the master said, "We have a fine house here," the house Negro would say, "Yes, our house is a fine house." Whenever the master said, "We," he said, "We." If the master said, "We have good food on our table," the house Negro would chime in and say, "Yes, we have plenty of food, boss, on our table." The house Negro would also indentify himself so closely with his master that when the master was sick the house Negro would say, "What's the matter, boss, we's sick?" When the master was sick *he* was sick. If the master's house caught on fire the house Negro would fight harder to put the flames out or keep the flames from enveloping the master's house than the master would himself. If someone were to come to the . . .

MODERATOR: He would naturally say, "We's sick," because the master was sick . . .

MALCOLM X: Oh yes, he would say, "We's sick" or "We's in trouble." If the master was in trouble, he would say, "Boss, we is sure in trouble."

MODERATOR: Well, I can understand where he might be in trouble if the master was in trouble, but I can't understand how he could be sick if the master was sick!

MALCOLM X: Oh, yes. This type of Negro loved the master so much—he never felt pain for himself; he only was in pain when his master was in pain. And this is very important to understand because you cannot understand the present-day twentieth century house Negro or twentieth century Uncle Tom until you have a real understanding of the Uncle Tom who lived on the plantation before the Emancipation Proclamation. And that type of Negro never identified himself with the other slaves. He always thought he was above the field Negroes. The field Negroes were the masses. The house Negroes were the minority whereas the field Negroes were in the majority. Now, sir, if someone came to that house Negro and said, "Let's separate, let's run," the house Negro would look at that person like he was crazy and tell him, "Run where? How would I live, how would I sleep if I leave my master's house? How would I eat if my master didn't feed me? How would I clothe myself if my master wasn't here to give me some clothes?" Well, that's the house Negro.

Now you have the other type of Negro—the field Negro. The field Negro was the one who really caught hell. He was the one who was dissatisfied. He was the one who was oppressed. He was the one who was downtrodden and exploited most. He was the one who felt the brunt of the master's whip, the lash of the master's whip—and he hated his master. If his master got sick, he didn't say, "Are we sick?" He prayed that his master would die. If his master's house caught on fire he prayed for a strong wind to come up and burn the plantation down. He never identified himself with his master in any way whatsoever. And if someone came to that Negro, that field Negro, that mass element, and said, "Let's go, let's separate, let's leave the master and strike out on our own," he wouldn't even ask where. He would leave. He wouldn't even ask you how. He would leave. He wouldn't ask you any questions at all. As soon as you said, "Come on, let's go," he'd be gone.

Now just as you have the house Negro and the field Negro a hundred years ago, in America today you have a house Negro and a field Negro. You have the modern counterpart of that slavery-time Uncle Tom, only the one today is a twentieth century Uncle Tom. He doesn't wear a handkerchief around his head, sir. He wears a top hat. He speaks with a Harvard accent or a Howard accent. Sometimes he is a lawyer or a judge or a doctor or he is an ambassador to the UN. He represents the government in all the international conferences. He runs to the Congo and tries to settle differences there, but he can't go to Mississippi and settle differences that his own people are confronted with in the face of these Mississippi southerners. This is the twentieth-century house Negro. He wants to live with his master. He wants to force his way into his master's neighborhood. He wants to force his way into his master's schools. He wants to force his way into his master's industry. He identifies himself with his master so much that when his master says, "Our society," he says, "Yes boss, our society." When his master says, "Our army, our armed forces," or "Our astronauts are floating around the earth," he says, "Yes." Now here is a Negro, mind you, talking about *his* astronauts floating around in space someplace or talking about *his* industry out here called General Motors or talking about *his* mayor in City Hall or *his* President in the White House. Every time the white man says, "We" that type of Negro says, "Yes, we." Now when he hears the white man say how rich we are, that Negro runs around talking about how rich we are, how enlightened we are, how educated we are, or this is the free world or this is a free country, and at the same time he is begging the white man for civil rights and integration and all that kind of stuff he doesn't have. He is a twentieth century Uncle Tom. He is a house Negro. He is no different from that house Negro during slavery other than that he is living in the twentieth century. But he identifies himself with the white man. He is never sick until the white man is sick. If you attack the white man, that Negro will open up his mouth to defend the white man better than the white man can defend himself.

Now then, you have the masses of black people in this country who are the offshoot of the field Negro, during slavery. They are the masses. They are the ones who are jobless. They are the last hired and the first fired. They are the ones who are forced to live in the ghetto and the slum. They are the ones who are not allowed to integrate. They are not the handpicked Negroes who benefit from token integration. They are not the bourgeoisie who get the crumbs that fall from the white man's table. They are not the ones who can slip into the White House or these big hotels when the doors are opened up. These are the ones who still are forced to live in the ghetto or forced to live in the slum or forced to get a third-rate education or forced to work in the worst form of job. They benefit in no way, shape, or form whatsoever from this thing that is called democracy. And that type of Negro—when you come to him—field Negro, this mass level type of so-called Negro—and tell him, "Let's separate," he doesn't ask you anything about "Where shall we go?" He doesn't question Mr. Muhammad's method of bringing about separation. He just says, "OK, let's separate. We are catching hell in this system we are in now. Let's separate." He has the same reaction to what The Honorable Elijah Muhammad is teaching today that the field Negroes would have if a man came during slavery and told those slaves, "Come on, let's go."

This was emphasized at the University of Pennsylvania today, to make the white people see that they are dealing with two different types of Negro. This integrationist Negro is the one who doesn't want to be black—he is ashamed to be black—and he knows that he can't be white. So he calls himself a Negro—an American Negro—which means he is neither black nor white. He doesn't want to be black and can't be white, so he is called a Negro. And since he is living in this American society he is always seeking a role for himself on the American stage. And since he knows that America is a white country and all of the economy, the politics, the civic life of America is controlled by the white man—the whole stage is controlled by the white man—whenever he sees himself on the American stage, he sees himself as a minority in the company of a white majority. So he is the underdog, and as an underdog he regards himself as a minority. He adopts the beggar role—the role of a beggar. And for everything that type of Negro seeks for himself he takes a begging attitude, a condescending attitude. So also, sir, he never looks at himself on the world stage. Usually his knowledge is limited to right here, to America, and he thinks of himself as an American in the American context which always keeps him in the role of a minority. But now when it comes to the international stage he can't see it. He is not interested in a role on the international stage. He only wants a minority role in America.

But there is another type of Negro on the scene. This type doesn't call himself a Negro. He calls himself a black man. He doesn't make any apology for his black skin. He doesn't make any apology for being in America because he knows he was brought here forcibly by the white man. It's the white man's fault that he is here. It's the white man who created the problem here in America that they call a race problem. This type of black man sees that. So he doesn't apologize for being here; he doesn't apologize for the problem that his presence confronts the white man with. He doesn't walk around bragging that he is an American or that he wants to be a part of the American society. This particular type of black man has been exposed to the teachings of The Honorable Elijah Muhammad, and having been exposed to the teachings of The Honorable Elijah Muhammad his thinking is international. He sees the world. He doesn't see America. He sees the entire world. And when he sees the world he sees that the majority of people on this earth are dark people and these dark people outnumber the whites. So he doesn't think of himself as a minority, but he thinks of himself as part of this vast dark majority who outnumber the whites, and therefore he doesn't have to beg the white man for anything. He takes his role on the international stage and that's not the role of a beggar, that's the role that he was automatically born for.

While I was at the University of Pennsylvania this afternoon, or this evening, I was trying to point out to them, to make them see the importance of recognizing the fact that there are two different types of Negroes in America today, and as long as they try and do business, we might say, only with this integrationist-type Negro, the problem can never be solved. We should take into consideration the fact that the Attorney General, Robert Kennedy, repeatedly, recently, has been pointing out that America's number one problem, domestic problem, is the race problem, and that failure to solve this problem is destroying America's image among the dark masses of Africa,

Asia, and Latin America. Also, failure to solve this problem has serious repercussions on the American economy,
as well as upon America's foreign policy. Even a recent
speech by the governor of North Carolina lends added
emphasis to the importance of solving this serious race
problem. North Carolina is a state where the so-called
Negro has been brutalized from the time he was brought
there, and even the governor of that state realizes the
importance of this race problem. So much so that that
governor was on television recently, pointing out to the
people of America the importance of doing something to
solve this problem. And then last week an interfaith religious conference of Protestant, Catholic, and Jewish
groups which was held in Chicago, dealing with the race
problem, that conference also broke up. And it broke up
with the problems of racism still unsolved. In fact when
one reads the results of that religious conference one has
to agree that it succeeded only in highlighting their inability to eliminate white racism from their own churches
and synagogues. So I was pointing out there at the University of Pennsylvania that no group or council or conference would ever solve the race problem until they
first recognized and included The Honorable Elijah Muhammad as an active participant in all of their discussions
and in all of their plans.

Why? Because The Honorable Elijah Muhammad is the
only black man in America who can speak for the oppressed and dissatisfied black masses who are impatient
and tired of sitting around and waiting for the white man
to make up his mind to do something to solve this problem.
Plus the fact that these other so-called Negro leaders that
are usually up in the white man's face are Negroes whom
the white man himself has set up as leaders, and they
don't represent any of the black masses. They don't speak

for the dissatisfied black people or the impatient black people. Usually they know exactly what the white man wants to hear them say, and they say it in the exact manner that the white man expects them to say it. And by listening to these Negroes the problem never gets solved, it only gets worse. Also, racial unrest never occurs among the satisfied, bourgeois class of Negroes. They can easily be appeased and controlled and influenced just by continuing to drop crumbs on their table—the crumbs of tokenism. And this type of Negro that the so-called Negro leadership represents is a type that can be appeased and can be controlled with the crumbs of token integration. But the racial explosions never take place among that type. Racial explosions always erupt among the oppressed, dissatisfied black masses, and The Honorable Elijah Muhammad is the only black man today that is speaking out in behalf of the black masses.

I read out there at the University of Pennsylvania an article that was in the *Detroit News* quoting a chaplain, Rev. Malcolm Boyd, a white Episcopalian chaplain at Wayne State University who pointed out that the conference in Chicago—the Interfaith Conference in Chicago—was a failure. In the *Detroit News* he said, and I quote him: "Although 650 leaders of American churches have gathered here, nothing has been brought out and nothing ever will unless the basic ideas of such a gathering as this are changed." The conference centered on the failure of religion to aid racial integration. Now Rev. Boyd pointed out, and again I quote: "My chief criticism was of the speakers selected to address the conference. They are leaders in the field of religion, highly articulate and persuasive, but they are not saying anything new or anything that will help solve the real problem for us."

Rev. Boyd believes that the conference might have accomplished much good if the speakers had included a white supremacist and a Negro race leader, preferably a top man in the American Black Muslim movement. And he went on to say, and I quote: "A debate between them (meaning this white racist and a Black Muslim) would undoubtedly be bitter, but it would accomplish one thing: it would get some of the real issues out into the open. In this conference we have not done that. The money spent to bring these people here has been wasted. We have done nothing to solve the race problem either in our churches or in our communities." Now the statements from this element that attended this interfaith conference on religion in Chicago have not been given wide coverage in the press. The press has used its outlet or its ability to reach the public to make the public think that an honest effort was put forth out there to listen to the gripes and grievances of the dissatisfied Negroes or to solve the problem. But those who attended admit, and the current *Jet* magazine points out, that the conference was a failure.

So all of this was put forth at the University of Pennsylvania, and it was pointed out to them that the only way the white man can solve his problem is to realize the existence of two different, distinct types of Negroes. This is the old type and the new type: that old type who is the Uncle Tom and wants to continue to beg white people to accept him or to force himself into the white society; then this new type of black man who wants to think for himself, speak for himself, stand on his own feet, and walk for himself. This type is following The Honorable Elijah Muhammad. If he is not an outright follower of The Honorable Elijah Muhammad he is in sympathy with the teachings of The Honorable Elijah Muhammad, and he believes that the only way our problem can be solved is that, instead of sitting around waiting for the white man to solve it, the black people have to come together. We have to forget our differences. We have to forget our religious differences, our economic differences, our social differences. We have to submerge our differences and get together behind the door and formulate some kind of plan, come to some kind of conclusions of what we can do to solve the problem of our ever increasing number of black people across the nation.

And it was also pointed out to the students at the University of Pennsylvania this afternoon that the only way they can understand the thinking of this new type of black man is to realize what he sees when he opens his eyes and looks around this world. And this new type of black man realizes that, in the past, dark mankind was ruled by white mankind. This is a fact. Right up until today, recent history, black, brown, red, and yellow man was ruled by the white man—which means European colonialism. This is what they call it, but in essence European colonialism meant that the white man was ruling the black, brown, red, and yellow people of this earth—which is, in reality, white supremacy. Now these same dark people who were ruled by the European minority were actually in the majority. It means that in the past the European minority, the white minority, was able to come together both by hook and by crook and rule the dark majority by practicing "divide and conquer."

When the black, brown, red, and yellow man of Africa and Asia realized what was going on, they had a conference in Indonesia which has come to be known as the Bandung Conference. And what they did at that Bandung Conference actually changed the course of history. They had many differences: they had religious differences, economic differences, all types of differences. But at the Bandung Conference the black, brown, red, and yellow man agreed to submerge their differences and come together against the common enemy, the thing that all of them had in common: that they were all being exploited by the white man, they were all being oppressed by the white man. They called him European, but actually he was a white man.

So once they reached a conclusion that they had oppression in common, exploitation in common, they were able to identify a common enemy, and this enabled them to unite against the common enemy; and out of this grew what we today know as the African-Asian-Arab bloc. They have differences among themselves, yet they work together. Their working unity enabled them to free the dark nations of Africa. The fast emerging independence of the nations in Africa has taken place since the Bandung Conference.

As these nations in Africa began to get their independence and come into the United Nations they had a vote, they had a voice, and they soon were able to outvote the white man, outvote the European, outvote the colonial powers. And by being able to outvote the colonial powers their vote was sufficient to produce a power that forced the people of Europe to turn loose the black man in Tanganyika, the black man in the Congo, the black man in what we today know as the former French West African territories. All of this stems from the unity of the black, brown, red, and yellow man in the United Nations. It created a new era. It created a new world. And it created a situation where the only people who were able to sit at the helm of the United Nations were no longer white or European or Christian or in the person of Trygve Lie or Dag Hammarskjöld or some of the others. Right after the black man, brown man, red man, yellow man agreed to submerge their differences and come together in unity, their unified force was sufficient to make it almost impossible today for a white man to be elected to the helm of the United Nations or for a Christian to be elected to the helm of the United Nations or for a European to be elected to the helm of the United Nations. Everyone that you see now sitting in the top seat of authority in the UN is either an African, an Asian, or an Arab, or he is either a Hindu, a Buddhist, or a Muslim. And all of this is the result of the ability of these black, brown, red, and yellow people to forget their little differences and come together against the common foe, against the common enemy, the oppressor.

And this is a good example that the black people in America can copy if we want to bring about freedom, justice, equality, and human dignity of the black people in this country.

It was also pointed out today at the University of Pennsylvania that The Honorable Elijah Muhammad's program is designed to make black, brown, red, and yellow people here in America, the so-called Negro, forget our differences. Any differences that we have we should take them behind the door, or any argument that we want to engage in among ourselves should be done behind the door. Instead, we need to present a common front against a common enemy, and the common enemy of the black, brown, red, and yellow man is anyone standing in the way of our freedom. Anyone standing in the way of our justice or equality. Anyone who deprives the black man in America of civil rights is an enemy to the black man. Anyone who deprives the black man of citizenship in America is an enemy to the black man. And when the black people in this country learn how to recognize the enemy, the common enemy, then the black people can get together in unity and harmony and do whatever is necessary to solve our own problems.

We won't be sitting around here waiting for the white man to issue some kind of emancipation proclamation. We won't be waiting for the Senate or Congress. We won't be waiting for any Supreme Court. Our unity will be sufficient to bring about human dignity, to bring about freedom, justice, and equality, and to bring about whatever the black man needs to enable him to stand on his own feet like a man.

It was also pointed out to them, so they wouldn't think hard of me in saying that their world was coming to an end, that their world was decreasing, that their power was on the downgrade, that they were losing out all over the world . . . I reminded them of a speech that was made by Prime Minister Macmillan on April 26, 1962, at the Waldorf-Astoria in New York City, to the leading publishers and editors of America, at which time Prime Minister Macmillan himself pointed out that in his own lifetime a change, a new world, has come into existence. He said that when he was a boy the world was a white world. Britain's power extended so far across this planet that they used to brag that the sun would never set on the British Empire. In Macmillan's own lifetime, the power of the Englishman, the white man in England, has decreased so much, or the British Empire has decreased so much, that today when the sun rises you can hardly find the British Empire.

And this is all symbolic of the decrease in power that the white man has suffered just in recent years. Just as Britain has dwindled down to nothing in prestige and influence in the face of the rising dark nations of this earth, all of your white nations have done the same thing.

France has dwindled down to nothing. She has lost her possessions in Asia and, after she lost her possessions in Asia, I think called Indo-China, it affected her economy so much that she didn't have enough strength, economic strength, to keep in existence an army large enough to dominate the large West African territories. She had to turn them loose, and finally she had to turn Algeria loose, just in our own lifetime, just in this present generation. Not only did this happen to England and France, but the Netherlands had to give up Indonesia. And as soon as the Netherlands turned loose the brown man's lands in Indonesia, the economy of the Netherlands dwindled down so that you hardly hear of the Dutch. You hardly hear of Belgium. Belgium used to be a power on this earth, as long as she could dictate to the black people in the Congo. But as soon as Belgium had to turn loose the Congolese, within a matter of months, the loss of the free and cheap mineral resources that the white man from Belgium in Europe was getting from the black man's lands in Africa affected the Belgium economy so much they had a collapse in the Belgium government. And all of this is a pattern that the white man's whole world, his whole kingdom, has had to face up to in recent times, during your and my generation.

So I pointed these things out to the white students at the University of Pennsylvania so that they could see themselves that their world is shrinking, that their world is coming to an end. And the thing that is bringing about an end to their world is the awakening of the dark world. As the dark world awakens, the dark world is rising. And as the dark world rises and increases, the power of the white world decreases. So when The Honorable Elijah Muhammad mentions to us, the so-called Negroes here in America, that we are living at the end of the world, all that means is that we are living at the end of the white world. When he says we are living at the end of time, all that means is that we are living at the end of the white man's time. The time that the white man could exercise unilateral and dictatorial power over the destiny of black people, brown people, red people, and yellow people on this earth has come to an end. And when The Honorable Elijah Muhammed says this they call him a black suprem- acist, they call him a racist, while at the same time in the halls of the United Nations Prime Minister Macmillan and all of the international diplomats are getting on the podium at the UN and crying the blues because they can see the handwriting on the wall.

And just like it took Daniel in Babylon to read the handwriting on the wall for that slave master or the de- scendants of Nebuchadnezzar, it takes The Honorable Elijah Muhammed, a little ex-slave here in America, to stand up here in this House of Bondage today and read the handwriting on the wall and let the white man know that his time is up, that his days are numbered, that he has been weighed in the balance and all of the seeds of injustice that he has sown in the past are coming home to plague him today. All of the injustices committed by past generations of whites . . . the present generation of Englishmen is suffering because it breaks them up to see themselves lose their empire. But still they are losing their empire because of seeds sown by their own foreparents in England and the present generation of Englishmen has to face that as a fact. The seeds of their forefathers have come home to plague this generation of Englishmen that live on this earth today.

Likewise, here in America, what has the American white man got to realize? That a crime was committed against the so-called Negro. And I think that the most important thing that was pointed out to the students of the University of Pennsylvania today was that a crime was committed against the so-called American Negro when our people were brought here. And today the white man, not realizing, not being capable of facing up to the fact, that a crime was actually committed, thinks he is doing the so-called Negro a favor when he opens the door to freedom. And I pointed out to the students: when someone sticks a knife into my back nine inches and then pulls it out six inches they haven't done me any favor. And if they pull that knife which they stuck in my back all the way out they still have not done me any favor. They should not have stabbed me in the back in the first place. Likewise, it was pointed out to them that when you take a man and frame him up, an innocent man and frame him up, and put him in prison—and because he rebels against this illegal and unjust framing and imprisonment he then is placed in solitary confinement within the prison to keep him from rebelling against the laws of the penal institution—after his spirit is broken in solitary confinement—why, the warden isn't doing that man any favor by taking him out of solitary confinement and then giving him more freedom within the confines of the prison wall. He shouldn't be imprisoned in the first place. And if they break down the prison walls completely and let that man out they still aren't doing that man any favor because they imprisoned him illegally and unjustly in the first place.

Now The Honorable Elijah Muhammad says that the white man captured millions of black people and brought us into prison, a prison house called America. They called it slavery; it was prison. And during the slavery or imprisonment of the black man in this country they inflicted the most extreme form of brutality against us to break our spirit, to break our will to resist, to destroy our manhood, to take the bone out of our back, to destroy our backbone. And after destroying our will, making us docile and humble, so that today we will turn the other cheek to those who are brutalizing us, after they did all of this to us for 310 years, then they come up with some so-called Emancipation Proclamation supposedly bringing us out of what we would call solitary confinement and giving us more freedom here within the prison walls of America.

And today the white man actually runs around here thinking he is doing the black people a favor because he gives us a little degree of freedom or justice or equality, or because he lets another one or two or three Negroes go to school with white people. The white man has the audacity to imply that he is doing black people a favor. What the white man should be made to realize is that his forefathers committed a crime by bringing our people here to this country. They committed a crime when they murdered our people throughout America. They committed a crime when they sold us from one plantation to another plantation like chattel or like merchandise or like common property. This was a crime and all of those crimes that were committed during the 310 years against the black people in this country are the crimes that have come home to roost today on this present generation of whites. And the only black man in America, the only black leader in America, the only black spokesman in America who will sit down and talk to the white man like a man, like a black man to a white man, and spell it out the way it is, is The Honorable Elijah Muhammad.

If the white man wants to solve his problem, if the white man wants to solve the race problem, if the white man wants to eliminate racial tension, then the white man should do the same thing that Pharaoh did who was the ruler of the House of Bondage in the days of Egypt. He was not able to solve his problem until he sat down and talked with Moses. Nebuchadnezzar wasn't able to solve his problems until he sat down and talked with Daniel. And today, here in America, this white man will never solve his problems until he sits down and talks with The Honorable Elijah Muhammad, and The Honorable Elijah Muhammad will tell him the same thing that Moses told Pharaoh: Let my people go. Not let my people integrate with you, but let my people separate from you. Let us go to ourselves and solve our own problems and build up some kind of society, some system, some kind of agricultural system, so that we can feed and clothe and shelter our own people, an economic system so that we can provide the necessities of life for our own people, and have our own government, our own flag, our own everything. The white man can stay to himself and we can stay to ourselves. Perhaps then we can get some kind of solution to the problem.

But they'll never solve the problem listening to these handpicked, Uncle Tom, bourgeois, upper-class Negroes whose only desire is to sit down in the white man's house or in the white man's neighborhood or in the white man's school. Some of them now even insist upon dying and being buried in the white man's cemetery. That's foolish, and the masses of black people in this country don't think that this in anyway is a solution to our problem.

So all of these things were pointed out to the students of the University of Pennsylvania this afternoon, not with any animosity or any hostility but in the language of frankness. And I think they listened very objectively and very intelligently. Sometimes there were little temporary disturbances by some—I guess they were white segrega-tionists (I don't know whether they were segregationists or integrationists)—who were sitting up in one part of the balcony. They were trying to do a little heckling, but it is impossible for a white man to heckle a Muslim. There is nothing that he can come up with that surprises a Muslim or in any way phases a Muslim. We are not interested in his heckling. All we are interested in is spelling out the problem. And if he is man enough to listen then perhaps he will get a better understanding of it.

So in this lecture this afternoon at the University of Pennsylvania, as well as the lecture at Michigan State University on Wednesday, our primary objective and purpose was to show the white man that just dealing with the integrationist-minded Negro will never solve the problem. If you read this week's *Jet*, the one that is on the newsstand right now, the observers who attended this interfaith religious conference in Chicago all agreed that it was impossible for the type of Negro leadership that was represented there to sit down and hold any kind of discussion with whites and really get to the root, to the nitty-gritty of the problem. The only way that the root of the problem can be gotten to is to have someone in those conferences who represents the masses.

You read about The Honorable Elijah Muhammad. One of the things that's always pointed out even by his critics is that the intellectual Negro doesn't follow Mr. Muhammad; they say that the educated Negro doesn't follow Mr. Muhammad; they say that the Negro with the high income bracket doesn't follow The Honorable Elijah Muhammad. What they always emphasize is that the only Negroes that follow Muhammad are those who don't have too much education, those who are oppressed, unemployed, and dissatisfied. Well, what they are doing right there, then, is admitting that it is the masses who follow The Honorable Elijah Muhammad, because the masses of black people in this country are unemployed. Even the job that they have is the same as no job, because their wages are so small that it is the same as not having any job at all.

Questions and Answers

QUESTIONER: Mr. Malcolm X says that we are so-called Negroes. I have been raised and taught that I am a Negro and now I have to file applications and they say what nationality are you. I would like for Mr. Malcolm X to tell me what shall I put down after this question when they ask me . . .

MALCOLM X: We put down Asiatic. Asiatic in this sense: The Honorable Elijah Muhammad teaches us that originally this entire planet today known as Earth was called Asia. When you read some of the so-called great historians they even point out that the entire earth was once known as Asia and all of the people on it at that time were Asiatic. The only people here were black, brown, red, and yellow. At that time there were no white people here at all. We refer to ourselves as the Asiatic black man. On my draft card it says Asiatic. And anything that anybody puts in front of me that wants to know what is my race or my nationality, any Muslim will put down Asiatic and that ends it. But never put down Negro. The worst thing that you can call yourself is a Negro. If you don't think so just call yourself that and immediately you will find all the doors closed. But at the same time the blackest man from Africa comes here and he rejects the term Negro. You can't call him a Negro. He will tell you he is an African and every door is open. Last year Kennedy made a special point in Maryland and Virginia to tell all those whites down there: don't do anything to practice discrimination against the African. Now at the same time he wouldn't make any statements concerning the American Negro, but he did come out and make a statement about the Africans. Which shows you that there is a difference between being Negro and being black. The African proudly calls himself black. But now when you call yourself a Negro that is when you encounter all these racial indignities.

QUESTIONER: The Muslims seem to have a great deal of answers to many of the problems that seem to surround the Negro neighborhoods. Now, why is it they don't have enough of their men who can go around, help work, and solve some of the problems, not only in Philadelphia, but nationwide. The Muslims seem to be doing a very fine job of recruiting men and turning them over from vice and crime into a better way of life. If the Negroes in our society who can see this group would come about to work with them, even if they don't follow a religious program, I think, as he said, we should put away our differences and seek a way to a better understanding.

MALCOLM X: That's a good question. An incident that happened recently right here in Philadelphia pretty well answers that. The local president of the local NAACP, Attorney Moore, came out and began to take a militant, uncompromising stand in behalf of the black people, and immediately he was accused of being a Muslim, from what I read in the paper. Instead of giving him credit for showing leadership, for showing the dynamic necessary to approach this problem and get it solved, all of the other elements, from what I understand, banded against him and attacked him. Now as Muslims it is an admitted fact by the critics of Mr. Muhammad that he is able to eliminate the vice, the immorality, the dope addiction. All the things they accuse the Negro of being guilty of, Mr. Muhammad is able to eliminate. And you would think that all these organizations would try to work with him. But instead of trying to work with him, as he would like to work with them, they can't do it because usually they don't have that much independence. Most of these Negro leaders have been put in their positions as leaders by the white man, and the only other black people that they can work with are black people who are approved also by the white man. And since the Muslims, Mr. Muhammad and his followers, are not on the approved list of the white man, this type of Negro leadership is afraid to openly identify or sympathize with what Mr. Muhammad is doing even though they know that what he is doing is good for the problems that our people are confronted with.

QUESTIONER: Sir, what I wanted to know is, being that he has just asked the question that the Muslims have men that will go out to work with organizations like NAACP regardless of religions, their creed—they won't accept these members of the Muslim sect to do this, would he suggest that those who are qualified should infiltrate and perhaps try to influence them in the religion of Muhammad?

MALCOLM X: He struck up a good point. I think you'll find, brother, that there are Muslims everywhere. Wherever you find militancy today among so-called Negroes, watch real closely. You're liable to be looking at a Muslim. This is by now what the white man is beginning to be afraid of. Every time he sees a Negro who speaks without compromise he swears that this man must be a Muslim. That's why I used Cecil Moore as an example. As long as you have a local man here in Philadelphia who can be maneuvered and manipulated and frightened by the white liberal, all these other Negro leaders will fall right in line and go along with him. But as soon as you get a black man who will stand up—I don't care whether he is in the NAACP or CORE or in any other organization—if he starts taking an uncompromising stand whether the white man likes it or not, you'll find that the Uncle Tom leadership will rally against him and classify him or charge him or signify or insinuate that he must be a Black Muslim. And you'll never make progress as long as you have those kinds of Negroes around. The only time the Negro leaders show any tendency in trying to get together in unity is when they want to attack another Negro. But those same Negroes who unite against one Negro, you can't get them to unite together on any problem under the sun except against another Negro.

SAME QUESTIONER: I feel that the American Negroes have enough money to get together and build, but they just won't do it. As you say, they'll fight each other and still bicker among themselves. So I can see what you are talking about there. But I also would like to know what he thinks about the real white man.

MODERATOR: I don't know what he means by the "real" white man. Is there an unreal white man?

MALCOLM X: The real one is probably the one he sees after his eyes come open. I might comment on something that he said that was very important, about the Negro having enough money to actually solve his problems. Anytime the so-called Negro has access to twenty billion dollars a year and you don't find him able to provide job opportunities himself, this is a sign of sickness. And The Honorable Elijah Muhammad says that if this so-called Negro would channel his wealth into business enterprises and create employment or create businesses that would provide employment then our problem would be solved. But as a rule, sir, in most Negro communities across the country the only thing you'll find Negroes building are Negro churches. An example: In Long Island the white man bought a city block. He built a huge supermarket on it. It creates job opportunities for about three or four hundred people. Now in the next block, believe it or not, the Negroes got together and bought it and built a million-dollar church. Now here this church provides a job only for the preacher; it provides clothing and shelter only for this Negro preacher. Now if this Negro preacher has the ingenuity that it takes to raise a million dollars or to finance a million-dollar project, but the only thing he can finance is a church, it's a problem. If you notice, white people in their neighborhoods build factories, they build schools, they build everything, and then they also build churches. But the Negro leadership, especially the religious leadership, has actually committed a crime almost in encouraging our people to build churches. But at the same time we never build schools; we never build factories; we never build businesses; we never build housing and things that will solve our problem.

QUESTIONER: Do you approve of the Cubans coming to this country when we have so much unemployment already?

MALCOLM X: I don't get involved in politics. But it does make the black people in this country who are jobless and unemployed and standing in the welfare line very much discouraged to see a government that can't solve our problem, can't provide job opportunities for us, and at the same time not only Cubans but Hungarians and every other type of white refugee imaginable can come to this country and get everything this government has to offer. But the Negro, this faithful soldier during wartime and servant during peace time, is always the last one in line when it comes to having some of his problems solved. It is not surprising that Hungarians and Polacks and Cubans can come to this country—who have never fought for this country, who have never contributed anything to this country's economy, who have never contributed to the defense of this democracy—can come here and get all the benefits of it. But the black man who has contributed with his life blood and his sweat for four hundred years is still the last hired and the first fired, and the only time they recognize him first is when it comes time to draft him into the army in defense of his country.

I think first things first. And the first law of nature is self-preservation. And we are interested in the black man in this country. And the white man—if he has got all that money to be given away all over the world—should be doing something toward correcting the condition that his own crime created when he brought our people here and made us slaves.

QUESTIONER: I would like Malcolm X to explain what he thinks about all this talk about birth control. Who is it for?

MALCOLM X: The white man is worried today the same way that Pharaoh was worried when you read the first chapter of Exodus in the Bible. The slaves under Pharaoh had begun to multiply so fast and Pharaoh and his people were almost becoming sterile. It tells you in there that because these Hebrew slaves were multiplying so fast Pharaoh had to devise a scheme whereby the fertile women and the babies that they were producing would be destroyed. And all this birth control that you hear the white man talking about today, it is not birth control. It is sterilization designed to make this productive, fertile black woman stop producing. As the previous listener pointed out, they never tell you the real number of black people in this country. When you look around here in Philadelphia and New York and Chicago and other cities why you can hardly go into any community without seeing a large number of black faces. Negroes are multiplying, they are increasing too swiftly. And just as Pharaoh had to do something to stop the growth of his slaves, today the American white man must do something to stop the rapid increase of the so-called Negroes. Already the Negro is the balance of power in any political election. The Negro holds the balance of power. In anything that goes on in this country, the ever increasing number of Negroes holds the balance of power. So something must be done to stop that growth or else it has to be controlled. And it cannot be done the legal way or ethical way so they use underhanded measures or underhanded methods in so doing.

QUESTIONER: I want to comment on the magazine article, number one. *The Saturday Evening Post* did the same thing when Nkrumah, if you'll remember, took over Ghana. He took the image of the Queen of England out of the Parliament. He took their image off his currency and he replaced them with their own portraits so that they could stimulate black honor and black dignity in their people. Now *The Saturday Evening Post* is doing the same thing now. That's one thing I want to point out. Now I want to ask Malcolm X this: Is it true that in your Elijah Muhammad speech two weeks ago you said that the struggle in the Congo was a struggle to recreate world colonialism and to control the resources of the Congo, because 86 and 2/10 percent of the copper is used in America and the gold deposits and also the stuff of which they make atomic bombs. If that is cut off America will suffer. And why are they spending $10,500,000 per month to kill people in Africa when they won't spend $10,500,000 a month to help the people right here in America?

MALCOLM X: Sir, you're a man after my own heart. I'm glad that you were able to see how the white press immediately turned against Nkrumah when they found out that they couldn't control him and use him as an agent as they use many others over there. And it is true that Katanga

Province is one of the richest sources of minerals, vital minerals, that exists on this earth. And if you were to do some research and find out who it is who has money invested in Katanga—some of them who are sitting in high positions in this government right now in this country, and some of them who are accepted by Negroes in this country as liberals in shining armor—when you find out who among the wealthy whites or powerful whites have money invested in the Congo or in Katanga, then you will see behind the struggle over there and why there is so much support for this man Tshombe and for trying to keep him in power. Anything you read in our newspaper, *Muhammad Speaks,* you can bet that it is true. If it wasn't truth they would stop us from printing it. And it is the only black paper in this country that will give you the raw truth that is taking place anywhere in which black people are involved on this earth. Did I answer all his questions?

MODERATOR: I think so. He used some figures.

MALCOLM X: It was true, and I wanted to point out, as a preacher, this man shows great intelligence in being able to analyze the news and show how the white press, as soon as the black man begins to take a militant and uncompromising stand, whether it be in America or Africa, will begin to project that man either as a dictator or as a black supremacist or teacher of hate.

QUESTIONER: I would like to know whether it is true that Malcolm X was arrested within the past four weeks and how much bond he had to pay to get out of jail.

MALCOLM X: I have never been arrested since I became a Muslim. What you are probably talking about is when two of our brothers were arrested in Times Square in New York on Christmas Day, selling newspapers, selling our newspaper in Times Square. In this particular paper there was an article about Congressman Nix, a local congressman from right here in this city, in which he himself took a stand, an open stand, against police brutality. And by the brothers selling the paper in the Times Square area a white policeman took offense and tried to stop them and arrested them and charged the two brothers with assaulting the cop. This is what police always do in cases of police brutality. They brutalize the black man and then turn around and charge the black man with attacking them. So we all went to court on that. But I didn't go as an arrested person. I went as a Muslim who was interested in seeing that my brother got justice. No sir, I have never been arrested since I have been a follower of The Honorable Elijah Muhammad. But that doesn't mean I am afraid to be arrested, and it doesn't mean that I am afraid of jail or prison. When it comes to telling the truth about what the white man is doing to the black people in this country I'll tell it and go to jail myself. They don't have to take me, I will go. So they can never hold that thing in front of me as a kind of threat. That is one of the things that the white man uses to make Negroes afraid to take a stand. You don't have to go behind bars to be in jail in this country. If you are born in this country with black skin you are already in jail, you are already confined, you are already watched over by a warden who poses as your mayor and poses as your governor and poses as your President. He is nothing but your warden keeping you in confinement. Don't ever talk that jail talk to me. I'll go faster than anybody in this country for the truth and be proud to go and be proud to die for the truth that The Honorable Elijah Muhammad is teaching us. And any other Muslim will be just as proud to do so, and will do it just as fast.

QUESTIONER: Mr. X claims that our spending power is about twenty billion dollars. Is that true?

MALCOLM X: Yes sir, according to the government economists.

SAME QUESTIONER: Well, all the speeches you make, or anyone else makes, is not going to make any difference in the world to the American Negro until he learns to hold onto that money. As fast as he gets it in his hands he runs around the corner and hands it back to the white man. The American Negro has got to put that money to use and build schools and build businesses . . .

MALCOLM X: Sir, I agree with everything you say. Everything you say is 100 percent true, and if you notice the Muslims have set up schools. If you'll read this *Saturday Evening Post* article, they don't like it. The white man doesn't like it but The Honorable Elijah Muhammad has set up a school in Detroit, a school in Chicago, and schools elsewhere, and it is in these schools that the racial dignity of the black man is taught to our children. We don't have any dropouts. We don't have any delinquency. We don't have any crime rate. We don't have the problems that the white man accuses the Negroes of allowing to exist in the Negro community. Insofar as the twenty billion dollars are concerned, we don't blame the white man because we are not able to take advantage of this money. We blame ourselves. And this is what The Honorable Elijah Muhammad says. That instead of us sitting around here begging the white man for a job in his factory or a house in his neighborhood, what we need to do is get together and unite. Pool our resources, pool our talent, and do something for ourselves. But what you have to understand is that the white man is afraid. The white man has a guilt complex and the white people today are so afraid since they know what they have done to the black people in this country. Their secret fear is that if the black man ever gets independent, if he ever gets able to stand on his own feet, the fear on the part of the whites is that you and I will retaliate against him. So the whites don't want the Negro to become involved in any kind of program that is going to make them independent of whites. They want the Negro to launch a program that the whites can still control or that the whites can still influence or in which they can still offer their guidance. But they do not want us to separate from them and go out on our own as The Honorable Elijah Muhammad is teaching us to.

QUESTIONER: What does Mr. X think about the Rev. Dr. Martin Luther King?

MALCOLM X: I think that any black man who goes among so-called Negroes today who are being brutalized, spit upon in the worst fashion imaginable, and teaches those Negroes to turn the other cheek, to suffer peacefully, or love their enemy is a traitor to the Negro. Everybody on this earth has the right to defend himself. Everybody on this earth who defends himself is respected. Now the only people who are encouraged to love their enemy is the American Negro. The only people who are encouraged to adopt this old passive resistance or wait-until-you-change-your-mind-and-then-let-me philosophy is the American Negro. And any man that propagates that kind of doctrine among Negroes is a traitor to those people. It is time for the black people in this country to come together and unite and do whatever is necessary to gain the recognition and respect of the world. And you know what Patrick Henry had to do to get some respect: He said liberty or death. He didn't talk any kind of peaceful suffering or passive resistance. George Washington didn't talk peaceful suffering or passive resistance. No hero who is respected by whites ever tried to propagate some kind of peaceful suffering or passive resistance. The Hungarian Freedom Fighters fought against the Russians. The odds

were against them. They were greatly outnumbered, the
odds were against them, but because they took a stand
and were willing to die for what they believed in, those
same freedom fighters can come to this country and get
respect and recognition and work on jobs and live in
communities that these Negro, what do you call 'em,
Freedom Riders, sit-inners, haven't been able to do yet.
So anytime you will show that you are willing to die for
what you believe then you will get respect and recognition
and this is what the black man has to learn. If it is all right
for black people to be drafted and sent to Korea or South
Vietnam or Laos or Berlin or someplace else to fight and
die for the white man, then there is nothing wrong with
that same black man doing the same thing when he is
under the brutality in this country at the hands of the
white man.

QUESTIONER: I was down South recently, in South Carolina, in Georgia, in Florida, and whatever the signs say
about desegregating, my wife and I were refused a bath-
room, we were refused liquor. What I want to know is:
Does he talk the same way down there as he does up here?

MALCOLM X: I preach what The Honorable Elijah Muhammad teaches me in Florida, Alabama, Louisiana, and
throughout the South. I am scheduled to be in Charlotte,
North Carolina, next Wednesday. I've been to Birmingham. We have a large mosque, a group of Muslims, in
Birmingham, in Tuscaloosa. No, the South is no different
from the North. Let me tell you the only difference. The
white man in the South is a wolf. You know where he
stands. When he opens his mouth and you see his teeth
he looks vicious. Well, the only difference between the
white man in the South and the white man in the North
is that one is a wolf and this one is a fox. The fox will
lynch you and you won't even know you have been

lynched. The fox will Jim Crow you and you don't even know you're Jim Crowed. And this is the basic difference between the southern white man and the northern white man.

MODERATOR: In other words, the northern white man is foxier than the southern white man.

MALCOLM X: He is foxy. When he opens his mouth and shows you his teeth you think he is smiling and when you look at a fox you think a fox is smiling, but actually the objective of the fox and the wolf is the same. They want to exploit you, they want to take advantage of you. Both are canine, both are dogs—there is no difference. Their methods might differ, but their objective is the same, and the southern white man and the northern white man are in the same category.

MODERATOR: To answer the gentleman's question, the answer is that you speak the same in the South as you do in the North.

MALCOLM X: Oh, yes, no different. Muslims speak the same everywhere, North, South, East, or West.

QUESTIONER: I want to ask Malcolm X . . . that he says it is the white man's fault that many of the Negroes have turned against Negroes by them going around killing each other, robbing from each other. And if I am correct I think you said that the white man had driven many of the Negroes to doing what they have done.

MALCOLM X: Oh definitely, definitely. When you see Negroes fighting and shooting and killing each other, all this is a throwback from slavery. There has always been open season on Negroes. A Negro can punch a white man in the mouth and the hunting season is always there. If you notice, sir, there is only a certain season when you can kill a bear or a rabbit . . .

MODERATOR: You have to have a license to kill an animal . . .

MALCOLM X: You have to have a license. But there are only certain seasons that you can kill that animal. But you don't need a license to kill a Negro and you can shoot one out of season—anytime—and you won't get any time. By Negroes knowing this, what the white man has done is set up a psychological situation where the average Negro thinks he can do anything to another Negro and get away with it. And this has made us antagonistic toward one another, hostile toward one another, and very disrespectful toward one another. And this is what makes Negroes continue to fight and kill each other.

QUESTIONER: I am a doctor in the city and this refers to the statements by Malcolm X about the white brutality against the Negroes and the general type of campaign which he seems to state that we have against the Negroes. A great deal of my time is spent in the emergency ward treating whites and blacks, and I must say that the greater percentage of patients who commit brutality to each other are the black to the black. Much of our time is spent suturing up these people, and treating very serious injuries, which shows the great brutality among themselves. And until they can show the whites that they treat themselves in a more humane fashion, I don't think they will develop the respect that they wish. The main thing I wish to say is that they should be improving themselves, as he stated, and they shouldn't speak of wanting money from government and whites, as he did in referring to the Cuban situation.

MALCOLM X: I think that the doctor brought out a very good point. It is true that Negroes kill Negroes but this is because the white man himself has taught Negroes to hate Negroes. The Negro hates another Negro because this was taught to us during slavery and the Negro hates everything about himself. And what The Honorable Elijah Muhammad is doing is teaching our people to love ourselves, respect ourselves, and uplift ourselves. And if the white man would realize that what The Honorable Elijah Muhammad is doing is actually correcting the myth that the white man has made, then the white man should stop harassing Mr. Muhammad and propagandizing against him and misrepresenting him in his news media, and instead thank him for the good work that he is doing.

MODERATOR: Thank you, Mr. Malcolm X.

God's Judgment of White America
(The Chickens Are Coming Home to Roost)

The Honorable Elijah Muhammad teaches us that as it was the evil sin of slavery that caused the downfall and destruction of ancient Egypt and Babylon, and of ancient Greece, as well as ancient Rome, so it was the evil sin of colonialism (slavery, nineteenth-century European style) that caused the collapse of the white nations in present-day Europe *as world powers.* Unbiased scholars and unbiased observers agree that the wealth and power of white Europe has rapidly declined during the nineteen-year period between World War II and today.

So we of this present generation are also witnessing how the enslavement of millions of black people in this country is now bringing White America to her hour of judgment, to her downfall as a respected nation. And even those Americans who are blinded by childlike patriotism can see that it is only a matter of time before White America too will be utterly destroyed by her own sins, and all

121

traces of her former glory will be removed from this planet forever.

The Honorable Elijah Muhammad teaches us that as it was divine will in the case of the destruction of the slave empires of the ancient and modern past, America's *judgment* and *destruction* will also be brought about by divine will and divine power. Just as ancient nations paid for their sins against humanity, White America must now pay for her sins against twenty-two million "Negroes." White America's worst crime is her hypocrisy and her deceit. White America pretends to ask herself: "What do these Negroes want?" White America knows that four hundred years of cruel bondage has made these twenty-two million ex-slaves too (mentally) blind to see what they really want.

White America should be asking herself: "What does God want for these twenty-two million ex-slaves?" Who will make White America know what God wants? Who will present God's plan to White America?

What is God's solution to the problem caused by the presence of twenty-two million unwanted ex-slaves here in America? And who will present God's solution?

We, the Muslims who follow The Honorable Elijah Muhammad, believe whole-heartedly in the God of justice. We believe in the Creator, whose divine power and laws of justice created and sustain the universe.

We believe in the all-wise Supreme Being: the great God who is called "Jehovah" by the monotheistic Hebrews. We do not believe in the Trinity (or "plurality of gods") as advocated by the polytheistic Christians. We who are Muslims call God by his true name: Allah, the great God of the universe, the Lord of all the worlds, the Master of the Day of Judgment.

The Honorable Elijah Muhammad teaches us that Allah

is the true name of the divine Supreme Being, and that Islam is an Arabic word which means complete submission to God's will, or obedience to God's guidance.

We who are Muslims believe in this religion that is described in the Arabic language by the word "Islam." This religion, Islam, teaches us submission to God's will and obedience to God's guidance. It gives us the moral discipline that makes it easy for us to walk the path of truth and righteousness.

"Muslim" is an Arabic word, and it describes a person whose religion is Islam. A Muslim is one who practices complete submission and obedience to God's will.

Here in America the word "Muslim" is westernized or anglicized and pronounced "Moslem." Muslim and Moslem are actually the same word. The true believers in Allah call themselves Muslims, but the nonbelieving infidels refer to Muslims as Moslems or Muhammadans. Many of the weak, backsliding Muslims who come to this country have also adopted some of these same pronunciations coined for them by the infidels.

But we don't condemn these "orthodox" Muslims, because the reward of the believer, as well as the chastisement of the nonbeliever and the backslider, come only from Allah. Allah is the only judge. He alone is master of this Day of Judgment in which we now live.

Why is the American white man so set against the twenty-two million "Negroes" learning about the religion of Islam? Islam is the religion that elevates the morals of the people who want to do right. Just by teaching us the religion of Islam, and by showing us how to live the life of a Muslim, The Honorable Elijah Muhammad is turning hundreds of thousands of American "Negroes" away from drunkenness, drug addiction, nicotine, stealing, lying, cheating, gambling, profanity, filth, fornication, adultery, and the many other acts of immorality that are almost inseparable from this indecent Western society.

The Honorable Elijah Muhammad has restored our cultural roots, our racial identity, our racial pride, and our racial confidence. He has given us the incentive and energy to stand on our own feet and walk for ourselves.

Just as we believe in one God, whose proper name is Allah, we believe also that this one God has only *one* religion, the religion of Islam. We believe that we are living in the time of "prophecy fulfillment," the time predicted by the ancient prophets of God, when this one God would use his one religion to establish one world here on earth—the world of Islam, or Muslim world . . . which only means: a world of universal brotherhood that will be based upon the principles of truth, freedom, justice, equality, righteousness, and peace.

But before God can set up his new world, the Muslim world, or world of Islam, which will be established on the principles of truth, peace, and brotherhood, God himself must first destroy this evil Western world, the white world . . . a wicked world, ruled by a race of devils, that preaches falsehood, practices slavery, and thrives on indecency and immorality.

You and I are living in that great Doomsday, the final hour, when the ancient prophets predicted that God himself would appear in person, in the flesh, and with divine power He would bring about the judgment and destruction of this present evil world.

The hour of judgment and doom is upon White America for the evil seeds of slavery and hypocrisy she has sown; and God himself has declared that no one shall escape the doom of this Western world, except those who accept Allah as God, Islam as his only religion, and The Honorable Elijah Muhammad as his Messenger to the twenty-two million ex-slaves here in America, twenty-two million "Negroes" who are referred to in the symbolism of the Scriptures as the Lost Sheep, the Lost Tribes, or the Lost People of God.

White America is doomed! God has declared that The Honorable Elijah Muhammad is your only means of escape. When you reject The Honorable Elijah Muhammad, when you refuse to hear his message or heed his warning, you are closing your only door of escape. When you cut yourself off from him, you cut yourself off from your only way out of the divine disaster that is fast approaching White America.

Before your pride causes you to harden your heart and further close your ears, and before your ignorance provokes laughter, search the Christian Scriptures. Search even the histories of other nations that sat in the same positions of wealth, power, and authority that these white Americans now hold . . . and see what *God* did to them. If God's unchanging laws of justice caught up with every one of the slave empires of the past, how dare you think White America can escape the harvest of unjust seeds planted by her white forefathers against our black forefathers here in this land of slavery!

According to the Scriptures, when God was going to destroy the wicked world with the flood, He first raised up a man named Noah, and missioned him as a warner to warn the wicked world that the flood was coming, and that he, Noah, was their only way out. . . . But their own wickedness and lust for evil made them too blind to see Noah, and they were thus destroyed by the flood of their own evil deeds.

Again, when God prepared to destroy the wicked world of the Sodomites with the fire of his wrath, He first raised up a man named Lot, and missioned him to warn the Sodomites of the fire that was coming to destroy them because of their evil deeds, and to let them know that Lot was their only way out. . . . But the Sodomites' addiction to their own lowly passions also made them too blind to see the divinity of Lot's mission and too deaf to heed his warning. They inherited the sea of fire and brimstone as reward for their rejection of God's servant.

Still later, when God prepared to turn his wrath upon the Egyptians, that House of Bondage, or Land of Slavery, God raised his servant Moses as a warner to the cruel slave master, Pharaoh.

Moses' message to the slave master was simple and clear: "Let my people go . . . Let them no longer be *segregated* by you; stop trying to deceive them with false promises of *integration* with you; let them *separate* themselves from you. Let them go with me to a place wherein the God of our forefathers has prepared a land for us . . . a land in which we can serve our own God, practice righteousness, and live in peace among our own kind."

And Moses warned Pharaoh: "If you will not let them *separate* from you and go with me, then our God will destroy you and your entire slave empire from the face of this earth."

Pharaoh's wealth and power made him too proud to listen to the little inarticulate ex-slave named Moses. He ridiculed Moses' lack of eloquence. White America's attitude today is the same toward The Honorable Elijah Muhammad. They ridicule him because of his lack of education and his cotton-field origin in Georgia. White America chooses to listen to the Negro civil rights leaders, the Big Six. Six puppets who have been trained by the whites in white institutions and then placed over our people by these same whites as "spokesmen" for our people. These handpicked "spokesmen" do nothing but parrot for the whites exactly what they know the whites want to hear.

Pharaoh used this same strategy to oppose Moses. Pharaoh also set up puppet-magicians to parrot his lies and to deceive the Hebrew slaves into thinking that Moses was a hate-teacher, an extremist, who was advocating violence and racial supremacy simply because Moses was trying to restore unto his people their own lost culture, their lost identity, their lost racial dignity . . . the same as The Honorable Elijah Muhammad is trying to do among the twenty-two million "Negro" slaves here in this modern House of Bondage today.

By opposing Moses, Pharaoh was actually opposing Moses' God; thus that same God (Jehovah) was forced to drown Pharaoh in the Red Sea, destroy his slave empire, and remove the Egyptian influence from the face of this earth.

History is repeating itself today. America now faces the same fate at the hands of Almighty God. That same divine handwriting is now on the walls of this modern American House of Bondage.

We, the Muslims who follow The Honorable Elijah Muhammad, believe that the symbolic stories in these ancient Scriptures paint a prophetic picture of today, of America, and of the twenty-two million "Negroes" here in America. . . . We believe that our present generation is witnessing the fulfillment of these divine prophecies, through the work being done among our people here in America today by The Honorable Elijah Muhammad.

This little, meek, humble, inarticulate ex-slave is a modern Noah, a modern Lot, a modern Moses . . . a modern Daniel.

In fact, he is a modern David, and like ancient David

The Honorable Elijah Muhammad has refused the carnal weapons of this wicked world and, armed only with a "slingshot" and "stones of truth," this modern David is battering the head of this modern Goliath (giant America), with a doctrine that no "helmet of falsehood" or "shield of deceit" can withstand . . . and it is only a matter of time, before The Honorable Elijah Muhammad's gospel of truth will make this American "giant of falsehood" topple and fall forever.

The Honorable Elijah Muhammad teaches us to believe in all of the prophets (including the prophet Jesus), all of the Scriptures, the resurrection of the dead (not the resurrection of the physical dead, but the resurrection of the mentally dead American Negroes); also Judgment Day and Doomsday (which only means: the judgment of this wicked world and its destruction by God himself).

The Honorable Elijah Muhammad teaches us not only the principles of Muslim belief but also the principles of Muslim practice:

1) We practice prayer toward the Holy City of Mecca five times daily.

2) We make charitable contributions toward the spread of Islam, or to spread this divine truth that will save our people from the destruction of this wicked Western world.

3) We practice fasting (we eat only one meal every twenty-four hours, and we abstain from *all food* for three days out of every month of the year . . . and we fast also during the holy month of Ramadan.)

4) Those of us who can afford it strive to make the pilgrimage to the Holy City, Mecca, at least once during our lifetime. The Honorable Elijah Muhammad and two of his sons made this trip in December of 1959, and others of his followers have been making it since then.

The Honorable Elijah Muhammad's mission as Messenger is to remind America that God has not forgotten America's crimes against his Long-Lost people, who have spent four hundred miserable years in this Land of Bondage. His mission is to warn America of the divine destruction that will soon rain down upon her from the very skies above her.

His mission is to warn America to repent, and to atone for her sins against God's people . . . or face complete destruction and permanent removal from the face of this earth . . . and removal not only as a nation but *removal even as a race!*

The Honorable Elijah Muhammad's divine mission, his message, and his work here in America is the same as that of Noah, Lot, Moses, and Daniel. He is a warner to our white oppressor, but a savior to the oppressed. He is preaching the divine execution of the wicked slave master (whom God can justifiably hold responsible for all sins); but he preaches forgiveness and salvation for the Negro ex-slaves, who have been made so deaf, dumb, and mentally blind by the slave master that no just God could now condemn these American Negroes for their sinful, ignorant behavior.

When The Honorable Elijah Muhammad says "end of the world," he does not mean the end of the earth; he is referring to the end of a race or "world of people," and *their* removal from this earth: the removal of *their* world.

There are many "worlds" here on this earth: the Buddhist world, Hindu world, Jewish world, Christian world —Capitalist world, Communist world, Socialist world— Eastern world and Western world—Oriental world and Occidental world—dark world and white world.

Which of these many worlds has come to the end of *its* rope, the end of *its* time? Look around you at all of the signs and you will agree that it is the end of time for the Western world, the European world, the Christian world, the white world.

The time is past when the white world can exercise unilateral authority and control over the dark world. The independence and power of the dark world is on the increase; the dark world is rising in wealth, power, prestige, and influence. It is the rise of the dark world that is causing the fall of the white world.

As the white man loses his power to oppress and exploit the dark world, the white man's own wealth (power or "world") decreases. His world is on its way down; it is on its way out . . . and it is the will and power of God himself that is bringing an end to the white world.

You and I were born at this turning point in history; we are witnessing the fulfillment of prophecy. Our present generation is witnessing the end of colonialism, Europeanism, Westernism, or "White-ism" . . . the end of white supremacy, the end of the evil white man's unjust rule.

I must repeat: The end of the world only means the end of a certain "power." The end of colonialism ends the world (or power) of the colonizer. The end of Europeanism ends the world (or power) of the European . . . and the end of "White-ism" ends the world (or power) of THE WHITE MAN.

Judgment day is the final hour when God himself sits in the seat of justice and judges these white nations (or the white world) according to the deeds they committed and the seeds they sowed when they themselves sat in the seat of power.

According to the Christian Bible, Judgment Day is that final hour when God will cause "those who led others into captivity to go into captivity themselves" . . . and "those who killed others with the sword to be killed by the sword of justice themselves."

Justice only means that the wicked slave master must reap the fruit (or harvest) of the evil seeds of slavery he has planted. This is justice! Other slave empires received justice, and now White America must receive justice. According to White America's own evil past, which is clearly recorded on the pages of history, so shall God judge her today.

Before God can bring about this divine destruction, He must first separate the innocent from the guilty, the righteous from the wicked, the oppressed from the oppressor, the exploited from the exploiter, the slaves from the slave master. God never integrates his people with those who are not his people.

The Scripture says God will separate his (black) sheep from the (white) goats, and the wheat from the tare. The goats are to be slaughtered and the tare cast to the burning flame . . . while the sheep are to be gathered into his pasture and the wheat into his barn.

In like manner God has prepared a Doomsday (a day of slaughter, a lake of fire) for this sinful white world of colonizers, enslavers, oppressors, exploiters, lynchers . . . and all others who refuse to repent and atone at the end of this white world.

God has also prepared a refuge, a haven of salvation, for those who will accept his last Messenger and heed his last warning.

White America is doomed! Death and devasting destruction hang at this very moment in the skies over America. But why must her divine execution take place? Is it too late for her to avoid this catastrophe?

All the prophets of the past listed America as number

one among the guilty nations that would be too proud, and too blind, to repent and atone when God's last Messenger is raised in her midst to warn her. America's last chance, her last warning, is coming from the lips of The Honorable Elijah Muhammad today. Accept him and be saved; reject him and be damned!

It is written that White America will reject him; it is also written that White America will be damned and doomed . . . and the prophets who make these prophecies are never wrong in their divine predictions.

White America refuses to study, reflect, and learn a lesson from history; ancient Egypt didn't have to be destroyed. It was her corrupt government, the crooked politicians, who caused her destruction. Pharaoh hired Hebrew magicians to try and fool their own people into thinking they would soon be integrated into the mainstream of that country's life. Pharaoh didn't want the Hebrews to listen to Moses' message of separation. Even in that day separation was God's solution to the "slave's problem." By opposing Moses, the magicians were actually choosing sides against the God of their own people.

In like manner, modern Negro magicians are hired by the American government to oppose The Honorable Elijah Muhammad today. They pose as Negro "leaders." They have been hired by this white government (white so-called liberals) to make our people here think that integration into this doomed white society will soon solve our problem.

The Honorable Elijah Muhammad warns us daily: The only permanent solution to America's race problem is the complete separation of these twenty-two million ex-slaves from our white slave master, and the return of these ex-slaves to our own land, where we can then live in peace and security among our own people.

The Honorable Elijah Muhammad warns us daily: The American government is trying to trick her twenty-two million ex-slaves with promises that she never intends to keep. The crooked politicians in the government are working with the Negro civil rights leaders, but not to solve the race problem. The greedy politicians who run this government give lip-service to the civil rights struggle only to further their own selfish interests. And their main interest as politicians is *to stay in power.*

In this deceitful American game of power politics, the Negroes (i.e., the race problem, the integration and civil rights issues) are nothing but tools, used by one group of whites called Liberals against another group of whites called Conservatives, either to get into power or to remain in power.

Among whites here in America, the political teams are no longer divided into Democrats and Republicans. The whites who are now struggling for control of the American political throne are divided into "liberal" and "conservative" camps. The white liberals from both parties cross party lines to work together toward the same goal, and white conservatives from both parties do likewise.

The white liberal differs from the white conservative only in one way: the liberal is more deceitful than the conservative. The liberal is more hypocritical than the conservative.

Both want power, but the white liberal is the one who has perfected the art of posing as the Negro's friend and benefactor; and by winning the friendship, allegiance, and support of the Negro, the white liberal is able to use the Negro as a pawn or tool in this political "football game" that is constantly raging between the white liberals and white conservatives.

Politically the American Negro is nothing but a football,

and the white liberals control this mentally dead ball through tricks of tokenism: false promises of integration and civil rights. In this profitable game of deceiving and exploiting the political potential of the American Negro, those white liberals have the willing cooperation of the Negro civil rights leaders. These "leaders" sell out our people for just a few crumbs of token recognition and token gains. These "leaders" are satisfied with token victories and token progress because they themselves are nothing but token leaders.

According to a *New York Herald-Tribune* editorial (dated February 5, 1960), out of eleven million qualified Negro voters, only 2,700,000 actually took time to vote. This means that, roughly speaking, only three million of the eleven million Negroes who are qualified to vote actually take an active part. The remaining eight million remain voluntarily inactive . . . *and yet this small (three million) minority of Negro voters hold the decisive edge in determining who will be the next President.*

If who will be the next President is influenced by only three million Negro voters, it is easy to understand why the presidential candidates of both political parties put on such a false show with the Civil Rights Bill and with false promises of integration. They must impress the three million voting Negroes who are the actual "integration seekers."

If such a fuss is made over these three million "integration seekers," what would presidential candidates have to do to appease the eight million nonvoting Negroes, if they ever decide to become politically active?

Who are the eight million nonvoting Negroes; what do *they* want, and why don't they vote?

The three million Negro voters are the so-called middle-class Negroes, referred to by the late Howard University sociologist, E. Franklin Frazier, as the "black bourgeoisie," who have been educated to think as patriotic "individualists," with no racial pride, and who therefore look forward hopefully to the future "integrated-*intermarried*" society promised them by the white liberals and the Negro "leaders." It is with this hope that the "integration-minded" three million remain an active part of the white-controlled political parties. But it must never be overlooked that these three million "integration seekers" are only a small minority of the eleven million potential Negro voters.

The eight million nonvoting Negroes are in the majority; they are the downtrodden black masses. The black masses have refused to vote, or to take part in politics, because they reject the Uncle Tom approach of the Negro leadership that has been handpicked for them by the white man.

These Uncle Tom leaders do not speak for the Negro majority; they don't speak for the black masses. They speak for the "black bourgeoisie," the brainwashed, white-minded, middle-class minority who are ashamed of black, and don't want to be identified with the black masses, and are therefore seeking to lose their "black identity" by mixing, mingling, intermarrying, and integrating with the white man.

The race problem can never be solved by listening to this white-minded minority. The white man should try to learn what the black masses want, and the only way to learn what the black masses want is by listening to the man who speaks for the black masses of America. The one man here in America who speaks for the downtrodden, dissatisfied black masses is this same man so many of our people are flocking to see and hear. This same Mr. Muhammad who is labeled by the white man as a black supremacist and as a racist.

If the three million white-minded Negroes are casting

their ballots for integration and intermarriage, what do the nonvoting black masses want? Find out what the black masses want, and then perhaps America's grave race problem can be solved.

Think how the late President himself got into office by only a scant margin which was "donated" to him by Negro voters, and think how many governors and other white politicians hold their seats (some by less than five thousand votes). Only then can you understand the importance of these white liberals place on *their* control of the Negro vote!

The white liberals hate The Honorable Elijah Muhammad because they know their present position in the power structure stems from their ability to deceive and to exploit the Negro, politically as well as economically.

They know that The Honorable Elijah Muhammad's divine message will make our people (1) wake up, (2) clean up, and (3) stand up. They know that once The Honorable Elijah Muhammad is able to resurrect the Negro from this mental grave of ignorance, by teaching him the truth about himself and his real enemy, the Negro will then be able to see and think for himself. Once the Negro learns to think for himself, he will no longer allow the white liberal to use him as a helpless football in the white man's crooked game of "power politics."

Let us examine briefly some of the tricky strategy used by white liberals to harness and exploit the political energies of the Negro.

The crooked politicians in Washington, D.C., purposely make a big noise over the proposed civil rights legislation. By blowing up the civil rights issue they skillfully add false importance to the Negro civil rights "leaders." Once the image of these Negro civil rights "leaders" has been blown up way beyond its proper proportion, these same Negro civil rights "leaders" are then used by white liberals to influence and control the Negro voters, all for the benefit of the white politicians who pose as liberals, who pose as friends of the Negro.

The white conservatives aren't friends of the Negro either, but they at least don't try to hide it. They are like wolves; they show their teeth in a snarl that keeps the Negro always aware of where he stands with them. But the white liberals are foxes, who also show their teeth to the Negro but pretend that they are smiling. The white liberals are more dangerous than the conservatives; they lure the Negro, and as the Negro runs from the growling wolf, he flees into the open jaws of the "smiling" fox.

The job of the Negro civil rights leader is to make the Negro forget that the wolf and the fox both belong to the family. Both are canines; and no matter which one of them the Negro places his trust in, he never ends up in the White House, but always in the doghouse.

The white liberals control the Negro and the Negro vote by controlling the Negro civil rights leaders. As long as they control the Negro civil rights leaders, they can also control and contain the Negro's struggle, and they can control the Negro's so-called revolt.

The Negro "revolution" is controlled by these foxy white liberals, by the government itself. But the *black revolution* is controlled only by God.

The black revolution is the struggle of the nonwhites of this earth against their white oppressors. The black revolution has swept white supremacy out of Africa, out of Asia, and is getting ready to sweep it out of Latin America. Revolutions are based upon *land*. Revolutionaries are the landless against the landlord. Revolutions are never peaceful, never loving, never nonviolent. Nor are they ever compromising. Revolutions are destructive and bloody. Revolutionaries don't compromise with the enemy; they don't even negotiate. Like the flood in Noah's day, revolution drowns all opposition, or like the fire in Lot's day, the black revolution burns everything that gets in its path.

America is the last stronghold of white supremacy. The black revolution, which is international in nature and scope, is sweeping down upon America like a raging forest fire. It is only a matter of time before America herself will be engulfed by the black flames, these black firebrands.

Whenever an uncontrollable forest fire is roaring down upon the farmhouse, the only way the farmer can fight that forest fire is by building a "backfire," a smaller fire that he himself can control. He then uses this "controlled fire" to fight the fire that is raging beyond his control.

Here in America, the black revolution (the "uncontrollable forest fire") is personified in the religious teachings, and the religious works, of The Honorable Elijah Muhammad. This great man of God cannot in any way be controlled by the white man, and he will not compromise in any way with the wrongs this government has inflicted upon our people.

The Negro "revolt" is controlled by the white man, the *white fox*. The Negro "revolution" is controlled by this white government. The leaders of the Negro "revolution" (the civil rights leaders) are all subsidized, influenced and controlled by the white liberals; and all of the demonstrations that are taking place in this country to desegregate lunch counters, theaters, public toilets, etc., are just artificial fires that have been ignited and fanned by the white liberals in the desperate hope that they can use this artificial revolution to fight off the *real* black revolution that has already swept white supremacy out of Africa, Asia, and is sweeping it out of Latin America . . . and is even now mainifesting itself also right here among the black masses in this country.

Can we prove that the Negro revolution is controlled by white liberals? Certainly!

Right after the Birmingham demonstrations, when the entire world had seen on television screens the police dogs, police clubs, and fire hoses brutalizing defenseless black women, children, and even babies, it was reported on page twenty-six in the May 15 issue of *The New York Times*, that the late President Kennedy and his brother, Attorney General Robert Kennedy, during a luncheon conference with several newspaper editors from the State of Alabama, had warned these editors that they must give at least some token gains to the moderate Negro leaders in order to enhance the image of these moderate Negro leaders in the eyesight of the black masses; otherwise the masses of Negroes might turn in the direction of Negro extremists. *And the late President named the Black Muslims as being foremost among the Negro extremist groups that he did not want Negroes to turn toward.*

In essence, the late President told these southern editors that he was trying to build up the weak image of the Negro civil rights leaders, in order to offset the strong religious image of the Muslim leader, The Honorable Elijah Muhammad. He wasn't giving these Negro leaders anything they deserved; but he was confessing the necessity of building them up, and propping them up, in order to hold the black masses in check, keep them in his grasp, and under his control.

The late President knew that once Negroes hear The Honorable Elijah Muhammad the white liberals will never

influence or control or misuse those Negroes for the benefit of the white liberals any more. So the late President was
faced with a desperate situation.

Martin Luther King's image had been shattered the
previous year when he failed to bring about desegregation
in Albany, Georgia. The other civil rights leaders had
also become fallen idols. The black masses across the
country at the grass roots level had already begun to take
their cases to the streets on their own. The government in
Washington knew that something had to be done to get
the rampaging Negroes back into the corral, back under
the control of the white liberals.

The government propaganda machine began encouraging Negroes to follow only what it called "responsible"
Negro leadership, and by "responsible" Negro leaders the
government actually meant, *Negro leaders who were responsible to the government,* and who could therefore be
controlled by the government, and be used by that same
government to control their impatient people.

The government knows that The Honorable Elijah
Muhammad is responsible only to God and can be controlled only by God. But this white government of America doesn't believe in God!

Let us review briefly what happened last spring: In
May in Birmingham, Negroes had erupted and retaliated
against the whites. During the many long weeks when the
police dogs and police clubs and the high-pressure water
hoses were brutalizing black women and children and
babies, and the Birmingham Negroes had called for the
government to intervene with Federal troops, the late
President did nothing but sit on his hands. He said there
was nothing he could do. But when Negroes in Birmingham exploded and began to defend themselves, the late
President *then* sent in Federal troops, not to defend the

Negroes, but to defend the whites against whom the Negroes had finally retaliated.

At this point, spontaneous demonstrations began taking place all over the country. At the grass roots level Negroes began to talk about marching on Washington, tying up the Congress, the Senate, the White House, and even the airport. They threatened to bring this government to a halt. This frightened the entire white power structure.

The late President called in the Negro civil rights leaders and told them to bring this "march" to a halt. The Negro civil rights leaders were forced to tell the late President that they couldn't stop the march because they hadn't started it. It was spontaneous, at the grass roots level across the country, and it had no leadership whatsoever.

When the late President saw that he couldn't stop the march, he joined it; he endorsed it; he welcomed it; he became a part of it; and it was he who put the six Negro civil rights leaders at the head of it. *It was he who made them the Big Six.*

How did he do it? How did *he* gain control of the March on Washington? A study of his shrewd strategy will give you a glimpse of the political genius with which the Kennedy family was ruling this country from the White House, and how they used the America Negro in all of their political schemes.

The late President endorsed the march; that should have been the tip-off. A few days later in New York City, at the Carlysle Hotel, a philanthropic society known as the Taconic Foundation, headed by a shrewd white liberal named Stephen Currier, called a meeting of the six civil rights leaders in an effort to bring unity of action and purpose among all the civil rights groups.

After Martin Luther King had been released from his

Birmingham jail cell in May, he traveled from coast to coast in a fund-raising campaign for his Southern Christian Leadership Conference. Roy Wilkins then began to attack King, accusing him of stirring up trouble, saying that after the NAACP would bail out King and the other demonstrators, then King would capitalize on the trouble by taking up all the money for his own organization, leaving the NAACP to hold the bag at a great financial loss.

As King, Wilkins, and other civil rights leaders began to fight publicly among themselves over the money they were trying to get from the white liberals, they were destroying their own leadership "image."

The white liberal, Stephen Currier, showed them how they were destroying themselves by attacks upon each other, and it was suggested that, since most of their divisions and disagreements stemmed from competition for funds from white liberals, they should unite their fund-raising efforts. Then they formed the Council for the United Civil Rights Leadership, under the pretext that it would be for fund-raising purposes. They chose the Urban League's Whitney Young as the chairman, and *the white liberal* Stephen Currier became the co-chairman.

It took the white man to bring those Negro leaders together and to unite them into one group. He let them select their own chairman, but he himself became the co-chairman. *This shrewd maneuver placed the white liberal and the Taconic Foundation in the position to exercise influence and control over the six civil rights leaders and, by working through them, to control the entire civil rights movement, including the March on Washington.*

(It also put the white liberals in a position to force the Big Six to come out against the recently proposed Christmas boycott by threatening to withdraw their financial support from the civil rights drive.)

According to the August 4 edition of *The New York Times*, $800,000 was split up between these six Negro civil rights leaders on June 19 at the Carlysle Hotel, and another $700,000 was promised to be given to them at a later date after the march was over, if everything went well with the march.

Public relations experts were made available to these "Six Big Negroes," and they were given access to the news media throughout the country. The press skillfully projected them as the leaders of the March on Washington, and as soon as the Big Six were looked upon in the public eye as the organizers of the march, and their image became inseparable from the march image, their first step was to invite four white "leaders" to become a part of the march "godhead." This group of leaders would supposedly okay all the plans and thereby control the "direction and the mood" of the march.

These four white "leaders" represented the same factions that had put the late President in the White House: Catholics, Jews, Labor, and Protestant liberals. When the late President had learned that he couldn't stop the march, he not only joined it himself but he encouraged all of his political bedfellows to join it. This is the way the white liberals took over the March on Washington, weakened its impact, and changed its course; *by changing the participants and the contents, they were able to change the very nature of the march itself.*

Example: If I have a cup of coffee that is too strong for me because it is too black, I weaken it by pouring cream into it. I integrate it with cream. If I keep pouring enough cream in the coffee, pretty soon the entire flavor of the coffee is changed; the very nature of the coffee is changed. If enough cream is poured in, eventually you don't even know that I had coffee in this cup. This is what happened with the March on Washington. The whites didn't integrate it; they *infiltrated* it. Whites joined it; they engulfed it; they became so much a part of it, it lost its original flavor. It ceased to be a black march; it ceased to be militant; it ceased to be angry; it ceased to be impatient. In fact, it ceased to be a march. It became a picnic, an outing with a festive, circuslike atmosphere . . . CLOWNS AND ALL.

The government had learned that in cases where the demonstrators are predominantly black, they are extremely militant, and ofttimes very violent. But to the same degree that whites participate, violence most times is decreased. The government knew that in cases wherein blacks were demonstrating all by themselves, those blacks are so dissatisfied, disenchanted, and angry at the white man that they will ofttimes strike back violently regardless of the odds or the consequences. The white government had learned that the only way to hold these black people in check is by joining them, by infiltrating their ranks disguised as integrationists; by integrating their marches and all their demonstrations, and weakening them: in this way only could they be held in check.

The government told the marchers what time to arrive in Washington, where to arrive, and how to arrive. The government then channeled them from the arrival point to the feet of a dead President, George Washington, and then let them march from there to the feet of another dead President, Abraham Lincoln.

The original black militants had planned to march on the White House, the Senate, and the Congress and to bring all political traffic on Capitol Hill to a halt, but the shrewd politicians in Washington, realizing that those original black militants could not be stopped, joined them. By joining the marchers, the white liberals were able to lead the marchers away from the White House, the Senate, the Congress, Capitol Hill, and *away from victory.* By keeping them marching from the Washington Monument to the Lincoln Monument, marching between the feet of two dead Presidents, they never reached the White House to see the then *living* president.

The entire march was controlled by the late President. The government in Washington had told the marchers what signs to carry, what songs to sing, what speeches to make, and what speeches not to make, and then told the marchers to be sure to get out of town by sundown . . . *and all of them were out of town by sundown.*

One of the Big Six leaders, John Lewis, chairman of the Student Non-Violent Coordinating Committee, was prevented from making a very militant speech. He wanted to attack the Kennedy administration for its hypocrisy on civil rights.

The speech was censored by the Rt. Rev. Patrick O'Boyle, the Catholic Archbishop of Washington, D.C. This was a case in which the Catholic Church itself, for whom Rev. O'Boyle speaks, put itself in the position of censoring the legitimate opinion of one of the Big Six Negro civil rights leaders.

The late President's shrewd strategy was: If you can't beat them, join them. The Catholic President placed his Catholic bishop in a strategic position to exercise censorship over any one of the Big Six Negro leaders who tried to deviate from the script in this great "extravaganza" called the March on Washington which the government had controlled right from the very beginning.

So, in the final analysis of the march: It would have to be classified as the best performance of the year; in fact it was the greatest performance of this century. It topped anything that Hollywood could have produced.

If we were going to give out Academy Awards in 1963, we would have to give the late President an Oscar for the "Best Producer of the Year"; and to the four white liberals who participated should go an Oscar as the "Best Actors of the Year," because they really acted like sincere liberals and fooled many Negroes. And to the six Negro civil rights leaders should go an Oscar for the "Best Supporting Cast," because they supported the late President in his entire act, and in his entire program.

Now that the show is over, the black masses are still without land, without jobs, and without homes . . . their Christian churches are still being bombed, their innocent little girls murdered. So what did the March on Washington accomplish? Nothing!

The late President has a bigger image as a liberal, the other whites who participated have bigger liberal images also, and the Negro civil rights leaders have now been permanently named the Big Six (because of their participation in the Big Fix?) . . . but the black masses are still unemployed, still starving, and still living in the slums . . . and, I might add, getting angrier and more explosive every day.

History must repeat itself! Because of America's evil deeds against these twenty-two million "Negroes," like Egypt and Babylon before her, America herself now stands before the "bar of justice." White America is now facing her Day of Judgment, and she can't escape because today God himself is the judge. God himself is now the administrator of justice, and God himself is to be her divine executor!

Is it possible for America to escape this divine disaster? If America can't atone for the crimes she has committed against the twenty-two million "Negroes," if she can't undo the evils she has brutally and mercilessly heaped upon our people these past four hundred years, then America has signed her own doom . . . and our own people would be foolish to accept her deceitful offers of integration into her doomed society at this late date!

How can America atone for her crimes? The Honorable Elijah Muhammad teaches us that a desegregated theater or lunch counter won't solve our problems. Better jobs won't even solve our problems. An integrated cup of coffee isn't sufficient pay for four hundred years of slave labor, and a better job in the white man's factory or position in his business is, at best, only a temporary solution. The only lasting or permanent solution is complete separation on some land that we can call our own.

The Honorable Elijah Muhammad teaches us that the race problem can easily be solved, just by sending these twenty-two million ex-slaves *back to our own homeland* where we can live in peace and harmony with our own kind. But this government should provide the transportation, plus everything else we need to get started again in our own country. This government should provide everything we need in machinery, materials, and finance; enough to last us for from twenty to twenty-five years, until we can become an independent people *in our own country*.

If this white government is afraid to let her twenty-two million ex-slaves go back to our country and to our own people, then America must set aside some separate territory here in the Western Hemisphere, where the two races can live apart from each other, since we certainly don't get along peacefully while we are here together.

The size of the territory can be judged according to our own population. If our people number one-seventh of

America's total population, then give us one-seventh of this land. We don't want any land in the desert, but where there is rain and much mineral wealth.

We want fertile, productive land on which we can farm and provide our own people with sufficient food, clothing, and shelter. This government must supply us with the machinery and other tools needed to dig into the earth. Give us everything we need for them for from twenty to twenty-five years, until we can produce and supply our own needs.

If we are a part of America, then part of what she is worth belongs to us. We will take our share and depart, then this white country can have peace. *What is her net worth?* Give us our share in gold and silver and let us depart and go back to our homeland in peace.

We want no integration with this wicked race that enslaved us. We want complete separation from this race of devils. But we should not be expected to leave America and go back to our homeland empty-handed. After four hundred years of slave labor, we have some back pay coming, a bill owed to us that must be collected.

If the government of White America truly repents of its sins against our people, *and atones by giving us our true share, only then can America save herself!*

But if America waits for Almighty God himself to step in and force her into a just settlement, God will take this entire continent away from her; and she will cease to exist as a nation. Her own Christian Scriptures warn her that when God comes He can give the "entire Kingdom to whomsoever He will" . . . which only means that the God of Justice on Judgment Day can give this entire continent to whomsoever He wills!

White America, wake up and take heed, before it is too late!